Get Started with Entrepreneurship

*EVERYTHING YOU NEED
TO KNOW ABOUT BUSINESS
TO BECOME A SUCCESSFUL
YOUNG ENTREPRENEUR*

First Edition

BY NICHOLAS TART

Founder of 14 Clicks

Fort Collins, CO

14 clicks

Feel free to use or republish excerpts from this book, as long as you link back to ***http://14clicks.com/*** *for attribution.*

And it's also okay to share this book in its entirety with friends, family, and anyone you think might be interested.
In fact, I'd be delighted.

Get Started with Entrepreneurship
By Nick Tart, *Founder of 14 Clicks*
Contributions from Nick Scheidies, *Founder of Newborn Collective*
Published by 14 Clicks

ISBN-10: 0-615-47245-1
ISBN-13: 978-0-615472-45-4

For more information about special discounts or bulk purchases, contact Nicholas Tart at nick@14clicks.com.

www.14clicks.com

CONTENTS

1

HAVE AN IDEA
SMALL, BIG, OR KOOKY

"All of my friends were doing babysitting jobs. I wanted money without the job."

ADAM HORWITZ
Made $1.5 Million in Three Days at 18

Mark Zuckerberg got the idea for Facebook while sitting in his dorm room. I got the idea for 14 Clicks while sitting in a coffee shop. You'll get the idea for your business while reading this chapter.

I'm going to walk you through brainstorming your idea, refining it, and packaging it for success.

By the end of this chapter, you won't just have your business idea – you'll know how to take the next step.

WHY START A BUSINESS?

"Young people in general must realize that here will be no better time to start a company than right now."

LAUREN AMARANTE

Co-Founder of World Entrepreneurship Day

Starting a business doesn't always sound like a lot of fun. Making money doing what you love? Now we're talking.

A **business** is a venture designed to make money. It involves selling a product or a service.

Entrepreneurship takes business one step further. An entrepreneur offers something innovative and scalable. An entrepreneur starts a business, makes money, hires people, grows, sells, and takes a long vacation. Then they do it all over again.

This book will show you how to become a successful entrepreneur.

Before you can start bringing home the Benjamins, you need to have an idea. Not just any idea: you need to find the right idea for you.

PICK YOUR PERFECT IDEA

"If you're not doing what you love to do, at least give it a chance… You're going to kick yourself in the butt for the rest of your life if you don't."

JOE PENNA
YouTube's Mystery Guitar Man

There's an art to picking the right business. Use this four-step process to find out what's right for you.

1. Find a Problem You're Passionate About

All good businesses solve problems. Before Google, it was hard to navigate the web. Before Facebook, it was difficult to stay connected with your friends. Before YouTube, it was practically impossible to upload and watch video online. Start a business that'll make people's lives better and you'll do just fine.

But don't pick an idea just because you think it will be profitable. If you don't love what you're doing, you're not going to put in the hard work to make it successful. Build your business around something that you truly enjoy. It's more fun that way.

We'll dig deeper into solving a problem in Chapter 3.

At 16 years old, Catherine Cook co-founded myYearbook with her brother David. They were both in high school at the time and there wasn't an easy and safe way for high schoolers to interact online. Since they were high schoolers themselves, they were passionate about solving this problem. They launched myYearbook.com at their high school in 2006 and now it hosts 22 million members.

2. Experience is Good, but Not Necessary

What are you good at? What are your skills? You'll find that you're most experienced in the things that you most love to do. If you want to start a business in an area where you don't have much experience, that's okay too. Everybody starts somewhere.

Joe Penna has the 6th most subscribed channel on YouTube (Mystery Guitar Man). But he wasn't always an amazing video editor. He told us, "I just watched the first video that I ever did, back in 2001. I cringed at every cut, like, 'Argh – why did I put a star wipe there? Not a good idea!' Everybody was bad at first. So keep at it."

3. Businesses Improve Quality of Life

The real trick is starting a business you're passionate about in a way that adds value to people's lives.

People aren't going to give you money unless you give them something of equal value. Don't ask, "How could I turn my jellybean expertise into a business?" Ask, "How could I use my jellybean expertise to help people?" If you can help people, the money will come.

Adding value to people's lives is easier said than done. But the good news is that people always want to improve their lives – no matter how many gadgets and gizmos we already have. If you're creative and determined, you'll find a way to do this with any passion – from painting to playing music to chatting with your friends on Facebook.

Mark Bao is the 17-year-old founder of 11 companies and three foundations. How has he found so much success so young? He told us, "My main goal is to create value for the customer."

4. Brainstorm Your Idea

Take out a piece of paper and write down five of your favorite hobbies, interests, or passions. Place a checkmark next to the ones that solve a problem.

Then brainstorm ideas why people would pay you to do something with that passion. Maybe you enjoy graphic design, playing with dogs, or making cosmetics. All of these hobbies can easily be turned into businesses.

Next figure out how you can provide a service around that hobby. Talk to a parent, friend, or mentor about your idea. If they think it's solid, sleep on it. If it's hard to sleep, it's a good idea. If you're still thinking about it in the morning, you're on to something.

If you're struggling to brainstorm ideas, push your creativity to the limit. Every passion has a problem. Every problem has a solution. Don't be afraid to experiment and write down outlandish ideas. It's just a piece of paper and outlandish ideas are sometimes the best ones.

At ten years old, Juliette Brindak started Miss O and Friends by drawing a few characters on a napkin during a family road trip. Nine years later, Procter & Gamble invested in her company at a valuation of $15 million.

Sell pain killers, not vitamins. It's much easier to get people to part with their money if they're purchasing something the need right now. If it's just something they want, they'll postpone the purchase.

PACKAGE YOUR BUSINESS

"You've got to stop doing all the things that people have tried, tested, and found out don't work."

MICHAEL DUNLOP

Founder of Retire@21 and IncomeDiary

There's more than one way to skin a cat. But who wants to do that? Below, we'll show you a couple of different ways you can shape your business.

Services are Easier to Start

Packaging your business as a service is great because you can start making money right away. You don't mow somebody's lawn until you know that they are going to pay you for it. Everybody has things they don't like to do – and they'll be willing to pay you for that service.

Ben Weissenstein started a service when he was 14. He and a friend went to their neighbors' houses and helped them with their garage sales while taking a cut of the profits. Grand Slam Garage Sales is now a national franchise.

Products are Easier to Grow

The only problem with services is that, as you become more successful, you have to keep serving more and more. 100 lawns can earn you a lot of money, but it's hard to find time or people to mow them all.

If you package your business as a product, you can earn money while you sleep. Get your product in local stores or put it up for sale online – and the money flows in without breaking a sweat.

However, a product will only be successful if it's great and great products require a lot of work up front.

I started a lawn mowing service at the age of 12. At 21, I found a way to transfer my lawn mowing knowledge into a product. With Emil Motycka, I wrote the Official JuniorBiz Lawn Mowing Guide, a product that we can sell anytime, anywhere.

> If possible, start your business as a service. Then expand that service into a product. This will allow you to earn money from the outset then scale up.

2

KNOW THE ROPES

CHECK OUT YOUR MARKET AND THEIR ALTERNATIVES

"You can't succeed as an entrepreneur if you don't know what the business world is about."

SABIRUL ISLAM

Best-Selling Author of *The World at Your Feet*

A good business changes and adapts quickly to its surroundings, like a monkey swinging through the trees. But that monkey is going to end up as panther-meat unless it knows the vines in the jungle like the hairs on the back of its hand.

You need to know the ropes for your business too – or you'll end up falling instead of swinging. The good news is that, unlike a monkey, you can read.

This chapter will guide you through the business jungle and, by the end, you'll be moving forward, confident in the direction of your business.

WHY KNOW THE ROPES

"Do the research. I didn't. Before you put your feet in the water, know where you want to go and how to get there. That's probably what I should have done in the first place."

JACOB CASS
Founder of Just Creative Design

Knowledge is good. Here are three reasons you need to look into your market:

1. **To see if your idea is worth your time.**
   Frankly, most businesses should never get started. People start with crummy ideas that don't have a chance to succeed and they ultimately fail. They still learn a lot in the process, but everything comes a lot easier if you start with a good idea. By doing a little research, you'll know if it's good or not.

2. **To find out how your industry works.**
   Every industry is unique. Basic business concepts can be applied to every industry, but you need to know the nuances of how your industry works.

3. **To discover your competition and potential mentors.**
   Competitors are your largest source of information. Pick through every nook and cranny of their business and don't be afraid to contact them. They might even become a mentor. You'll learn more from your competitors and mentors than any class you could ever take or book you could ever read.

YOUR MARKET AND COMPETITION

"The first thing somebody needs to do when they come up with an entrepreneurial idea is question why it hasn't been done before."

PHILIP HARTMAN
2008 Young Inventor of the Year

It's tempting to jump right in with your business, but that's like entering an obstacle course blindfolded. Here's how to get a better grasp of your surroundings.

Google Your Idea

The internet enables you to scan the entire world for traces of your idea. It only takes a few minutes to type in some keywords and scan the results for useful information.

When Lauren Amarante first got the idea for World Entrepreneurship Day, she immediately searched online to see if someone else had already done it. She was "thrilled to discover that there wasn't already one," and – just like that – World Entrepreneurship Day was born.

Write down the words you searched for when trying to find people who are doing your idea. These will be the keywords you will use when making your website to get search engine traffic.

Phone Books are Actually Useful

If your business is focused on the local market, then a phone book is a surprisingly great resource. All of your competitors are grouped within a few pages of each other. In a matter of minutes, you can get all of their contact information, learn about their business models, and see the words that they use in their ads to lure customers.

> If you have a lawn maintenance service (like Emil Motycka) and you're looking to expand it, then a phone book provides a comprehensive list of your competitors. Feel free to give them a call or pay them a visit: you're sure to learn something about the local market.

Finding Competitors is Good

There wouldn't be competitors if there was nothing to compete over. Competition means that people are paying for the solution that you're going to offer. Of course, this means you have to set yourself apart, but we'll get more into that in Chapter 4.

> When Catherine Cook and her brother started myYearbook.com in 2005, they were high school kids. They couldn't have had bigger competition: MySpace and Facebook. But big competition also means a big market – and today myYearbook.com makes $20 million annually.

Learn from What They're Doing

Your competition is one of your greatest resources. Subscribe to their newsletters and you'll be privy to the inner workings of their business. Figure out the answers to these questions:

- How did they get started?

- How are they attracting customers? Who is their target market?

- How much are they charging?

- How is their product or service similar to what you want to do? Different?

- How do they use their website to capture sales leads?

> Here's what Catherine Cook had to say about learning from Facebook: "If your competitor is a big player, you need to pay attention to what they're doing and learn from it. Otherwise, you're going into the market blind."

How to Contact Your Competition

If you want to be bold, contact your competition and ask for help. Start by collecting contact information (preferably phone numbers) of five of your competitors. Have a list of five questions you'd like to ask each of them (you can choose a few from the previous list) and call them up.

Speak to the business owner because to get the best advice. Ask if they have a few minutes to help you out. If they do, ask away. Write down their answers. Rinse and repeat.

Use this conversation script if you're nervous:

[Ring… Ring…]

Them: "Hi, this is Bizzy McBizzerson with 14 Clicks. How may I help you?"

You: "Hi Bizzy! My name is [your name] and I'm an entrepreneur who is interested in learning more about [their industry/market/business]. Can you put me in touch with the owner of [their company]?"

Them: "Yeah, I'm the owner." or "Sure thing. His name is Nick Tart. Let me redirect you."

You: "Great! Do you have a moment for a few questions?" or "Hi Nick! My name is [your name] and I'm a young entrepreneur who is interested in learning more about [their industry/market/business]. Do you have a moment for a few questions?"

Them: "I sure do! Hit meh!"

You: [Ask away!]

Last summer, I taught an entrepreneurship class to a group of disadvantaged youth. One of them, Robert, wanted to open a night club. I challenged all of them to call a competitor. Robert was the only one who did. He used my phone to call the biggest night club in San Diego. I can't wait to show up at his night club one day.

> Always smile when you're talking to someone, even on the phone. Your smile makes your voice more pleasant. It'll make people feel more comfortable talking to you and more likely to reveal their secrets.

Your Competitors Might Not Be Obvious

Keep in mind that you're competing against every alternative that they have, not just similar companies. For instance, if you have a service, one of your competitors is the customer doing the job themselves.

Philip Hartman is the 15-year-old inventor of the Steam Tech, a device that emits steam onto a car's windshield to defrost it in 15 seconds. The technology is so innovative that Philip has no direct competition. However, he still has to compete with normal windshield wipers and people who prefer to hang outside their window to clean it with a rag.

Contact Potential Customers

The absolute best source of feedback and advice for your business is potential customers. They'll know exactly what they want, how they want to get it, and how much they'll pay for it.

Just make sure you approach the conversation as someone who is only looking for feedback. Don't transition the conversation into, "Would you like to buy?" If they would, they'll let you know.

Catherine Cook developed all the tools for myYearbook.com by asking all of her friends what they wanted in a website. If she thought a part of the website would be cool but found out that nobody wanted it, they didn't waste time developing it.

More Due Diligence on Your Industry

Going through the steps above will be sufficient for getting you started. But if you want to increase your chances of success (and don't mind putting in a little extra work), you can do these two things:

1. **Find the NAICS and SICS codes.**
   Every industry is classified by NAICS and SICS. Find the codes for your industry so you'll be able to research more statistics about the past, present, and future outlook of your market. Find your industry codes at www.naics.com/search.htm.

2. **Learn more about your industry.**
   Once you know the codes, you can look up stats about your industry at **Ibisworld** or **Hoovers** (might need a subscription to use these sites). The stats will tell you the size of the industry and whether or not it's growing.

When I wrote my business plan for JuniorBiz I had to find the NAICS code. None of them fit perfectly but I settled on the Internet Publishing Industry (NAICS 519130). According to the US Census Bureau, revenue growth was 19% in 2008.

Be wary. Maybe your idea has little competition because there's no market for it. At this stage, give your idea the once-over to make sure that it has a solid chance to succeed.

FIND YOUR MENTORS

"Most students, me included, have a clouded vision of the world. Certain mentors can open it up and show you something completely different."

LAUREN AMARANTE
Co-Founder of World Entrepreneurship Day

Mentors are people who've been there and done that. They've made business mistakes so you don't have to. A good mentor is one of the most valuable assets you can have.

Look for the Experts in Your Field

When you were checking out your competition, you probably caught the names of a few heavy-hitters in your field. See if you can find interviews with them, or grab their email address from the contact page.

> Adam Toren, cofounder of YoungEntrepreneur.com, is the expert in our field. Luckily for us, he's a nice guy who's generous with his time and advice. He's been a great resource to help me bring 14 Clicks and *What it Takes to Make More Money than Your Parents* to a bigger audience.

Offer Something for Free

It's easier to get some face-time with a mentor when you make it irresistible for them to meet with you. Offer up your skills as a web designer, a writer, or an errand-runner. They'll probably be happy to take your assistance.

Otherwise, you can always offer to take them out to lunch. Everybody eats – and it's a cheap way to make a very valuable connection.

> 20-year-old Marshall Haas emailed AJ Vaynerchuk of VaynerMedia and asked him if he'd sit down for lunch in New York City. The only problem: Marshall lives in Dallas. Once he scheduled the lunch, Marshall bought a plane ticket and flew out to

the Big Apple to build a relationship with AJ. It paid off. VaynerMedia offered him a hard-to-come-by internship (which Marshall ended up turning down to focus on his business).

How to Contact and Meet a Mentor

It's time to send an email to your mentor-to-be and schedule a 20-minute chat. Not everybody is going to respond to your email, but you'll be surprised by how many big shots are eager to help upstart entrepreneurs like you.

Once you've found the expert(s) in your field, research everything you can about them. Start by looking them up on LinkedIn.com. If they're a good potential mentor, they'll have a profile with links to all their projects and information about their entire career.

Pull out interesting facts or tidbits that you can use to impress them. Then develop a few ideas of how you can help them.

Use this script to send them an email:

Hi Mr./Mrs.[Last Name],

My name is [Your Full Name] and I've spent the last hour on your website trying to learn everything I can about what you're doing with [Their Company]. I'm particularly impressed with how you [interesting tidbit that you found].

Anyway, there's a lot I want to learn from you. So I've brainstormed a few ideas on how I can help you. Can we schedule 20 minutes to talk next week so I can run these ideas by you?

Please let me know when you're available.

Looking forward to your response,

[Your Full Name]

[Your Contact Info]

One of Emil Motycka's mentors is John Malone. With a net worth of $3 Billion, John Malone is the 110th wealthiest person in the world. Emil won this mentorship through a high school entrepreneurship competition. When he wants to meet with his mentor, Emil sends an email to John Malone's secretary.

You may feel like a nuisance when you ask for help, but don't. Think of yourself as an engaging, up-and-comer who presents a great opportunity for the mentor to help out – and your mentor will likely think of you in the same light.

RECRUIT YOUR TEAM

"You also have to understand that you can't do it all by yourself. Business is a team project."

STANLEY TANG
Instant Amazon Best-Seller at 14

Tom Brady was crowned the MVP of the 2010/2011 football season, but he didn't end it with a ring.

It's hard to win championships and leave legacies by yourself, but you can't do it with a crummy team either.

Fly Solo

If you're starting a business for the first time, it's best to start it by yourself. When you have partners, you have to manage them; they all have to have the same vision; they need to be just as dedicated; and the legalities of a partnership are more complicated.

Once you've validated your business and proven yourself as a business person, then you can hire and motivate people as partners or employees.

Jacob Cass has always done everything himself for his graphic design service. When you're providing a service as an artist, it's nearly impossible to find people to do the work for you. But his company isn't going to grow much until he does.

Soar with Partners

The first step in recruiting partners is to find a diverse group of people who have the time and desire to be part of your team. An ideal team is three or four people. Starting with more is hard to manage.

Once you have your partners on board, it's time to set roles. There are three primary roles that your team needs to fill:

1. **Chief Executive Officer (CEO)**
   Someone, probably you, needs to be the team leader and ultimate decision maker. This person establishes project goals, sets deadlines, and delegates tasks. They also make the final decisions for the business. The CEO should have experience managing people and a charismatic personality that people want to follow.

2. **Chief Marketing Officer (CMO)**
   This person is responsible for all the marketing and sales. They'll help to establish and manage the brand identity for your company. Then they become responsible for bringing in customers. The CMO should have a marketing background and a natural talent for selling.

3. **Product Developer or Service Provider**
   This person is the engine of the business. They're role isn't as glamorous as the first two, but the company doesn't move without them. They are responsible for creating and providing the products and services that your company sells. As you bring in more people, this is where they'll start.

The last thing you need to settle with your team is the compensation. As long as everyone is contributing equally, the easiest way to do that is to split ownership between each team member. If you don't want to do that, find another way to compensate them. But they're not going to be gung-ho for the business like you if don't pay them what they're worth.

Emil Motycka started a lawn mowing company when he was nine years old. He ran it by himself until he was a senior in high school. Up to that point, he was maxed out at about 80 lawns per week. Now at 22, he has a small team working for him. His company serviced 200+ lawns per week in 2010 and he only mowed a few lawns himself.

The product developers and service providers will do the majority of the work that makes money for the company, but all of the roles are contributing equally to make the company run. If you take the CEO position, one of your responsibilities is to communicate this to every team member so they don't get frustrated with their   roles.

3

PLAN YOUR SUCCESS

DISCOVER HOW YOU'LL MAKE MONEY

"Realizing that anyone can do it is the first step. The next step is figuring out how you're going to do it."

ADORA SVITAK

Two-Time Published Author by Age 12

R emember those two explorers who tried to cross the Pacific without food, water, or sails? Neither do we – because they died before they got to Hawaii.

You wouldn't set out on the high seas without a plan and you shouldn't start a business without one either. That's why we asked every young entrepreneur we interviewed to give us advice about how to plan a business when just starting out.

A lot of that advice is below. By the time you finish this chapter you'll have an idea of where you're going and how you'll get there.

WHAT PROBLEM YOU SOLVIN'?

"My main goal is to create value for the customer."

MARK BAO

11 Companies and 3 Foundations by 17

Every good business solves a problem. Lemonade stands do well because people get thirsty. Knowing the core problem that you'll be solving is vital to the success of your business.

The problem and your solution will be the first thing you tell people when they ask you about your business. It'll drive your mission and be plastered all over your marketing materials (e.g. "I realized [this problem]. I'm fixing it by…").

If you don't know what problem your business is solving, then you need to figure it out right now.

In our case, there are a lot of young people struggling to find their purpose in life. 69% of them want to turn to entrepreneurship. Either they don't know how or they get started and 93% of them fail within two years. That's a huge problem. We want to solve it by giving young people the resources and tools they need to become successful entrepreneurs.

> All businesses start by solving a problem. The bigger the problem, the bigger the opportunity. But it'll be hard to compete if another company is already doing a great job of solving the problem.

WHAT YOU SELLIN'?

"Come to India. Go to the streets. They are street-smart people. They know how to sell. They can sell you your own shoes in two minutes."

KING SIDHARTH
19-Year-Old Entrepreneur from India

A good salesperson can sell somebody their own shoes. Luckily, you don't have to be that good. Here I'll break down how to present your product or service in a way that makes it irresistible.

Hint: you're not selling a product or service.

What is Your Product or Service?

You know your product or service like the back of your hand, but your potential customers are clueless. You need to clearly explain the features of your product and the attributes of your service. They're not going to put their hard-earned cash in your wallet unless they believe that they're problem will be fixed by what you're offering.

Our book, *50 Interviews: Young Entrepreneurs (Vol. 1) - What it Takes to Make More Money than Your Parents*, has its feature right at the beginning of our title. It has interviews with young entrepreneurs. We wanted everyone to know that from the get-go.

Why is Yours Better than Alternatives?

Have you ever seen those Tide commercials where they claim that their laundry detergent gets your clothes brighter, fresher, and softer than the competition?

The words "brighter, fresher, and softer" tell you why you need Tide more than the alternatives. When you tell people about your product or service, think about how you can demonstrate the ways it is better than the rest.

> Check out the subtitle of our book: *The world's top young entrepreneurs share the secrets to their success.* Our book is better than other books because it has the collective secrets from the top young entrepreneurs in the world.

What's the Benefit to the Customer?

The reason someone buys something is because that product or service is going to make their life better. You need to give them a clear benefit, a reason to buy. Why are you the right answer, solution, and investment for them?

You're selling benefits, not features or advantages. Benefits solve the customers' pain. Identify their frustration and how your business solves it. People purchase emotionally and justify their decision rationally.

> Our book title is designed to demonstrate the benefit of reading our book. It's going to reveal *What it Takes to Make More Money than Your Parents*. With that, we've squeezed the feature, advantage, and benefit of our book on the cover.

Research and Development (R&D)

Once you've nailed down your features, advantages, and benefits (FAB), start thinking about how you're going to develop the right product or service. Before you start sketching it up, you need to build the foundation of your marketing.

So we'll talk more about R&D in Chapter 7.

> The trick to balancing cockiness and humbleness is confidence. Don't be cocky or people won't like you, trust you, or want to buy what you're selling. Don't be purely humble or people won't take you seriously. Just

be confident. If you lean in one direction, always lean towards humility.

DETERMINE STARTUP COSTS

"When I started Grand Slam Garage Sales with my friend Matt, we went to Walmart and bought two red polo shirts [as uniforms] for about eight dollars apiece."

BEN WEISSENSTEIN
Founder of Grand Slam Garage Sales

If your only start-up costs are a couple of polo shirts, consider yourself lucky.

In any case, you need to know how much your business is going to cost to get off the ground. You don't want to be blindsided with an unexpected expense or an empty wallet.

What do You Need to Start?

Every business needs something in order to get started. It could be a tool, like a lawn mower or a truck. It could be a product, like a batch of brownies or a book. And it could be something that you can't touch, like a website or an education.

Before Joe Penna dropped out of medical school, he made sure that he had everything he needed to start a successful YouTube channel: a camera, video editing software, video editing expertise, and – in his case – a pair of black sunglasses.

Double Your Estimated Costs

Starting a business generally costs about twice as much as you think. There are unexpected challenges and expenses lurking around every corner. To be on the safe side, double your estimated costs.

We thought that we had all of our bases covered with the publishing and promotion of our book. That was before we were blindsided by additional expenses, like a publishing revision fee, an Aweber email marketing subscription, cover redesign, shipping materials, video recording software, and plane tickets to Chicago (all told about $1150).

Always, Always Bootstrap

Entrepreneurs have to pull themselves up by their bootstraps. Find ways to get your business up and running as cheaply as possible.

Every expense is an opportunity to find a way to get something done at a better price. Always research the best option, focus on efficiency, and don't be afraid to ask about discounts.

Today, Joe Penna lives comfortably on the money he earns through his YouTube channel. When he first moved to Los Angeles he was making $900 a month and his rent was $850. As early as January 2010, he was still sleeping on the floor of his apartment because he couldn't afford furniture. In his case, his biggest expenses were the daily needs of life. Joe's bootstrapping solution: Ramen Noodles.

> Start by making a list with all of the things you need. Then, look for used items and student discounts. Some good places to start are Craigslist, Half.com, and Ebay.

SETTLE ON YOUR PRICING

"Initially, they are hiring you for the price. But after you form that relationship, they are hiring you for you – and that is what gives your company value."

EMIL MOTYCKA

From 'Mow Boy' to $250K

Pricing your product or service is hard. A low price will help you attract more customers and earn more market share. A higher price will increase your profit margins but result in a lower sales volume.

This section will help you make like Goldilocks and find your "just right." Then I'll show you how to predict the day that your business will be profitable.

What does it Cost You?

Maybe you'd like to sell your product for five dollars, so you can sell it to as many people as possible – but that's not going to fly if the product costs six dollars to make.

The first thing to think about when pricing is what your product is going to cost you, in dollars, minutes, and energy.

> When Emil Motycka started mowing lawns as a nine-year-old, he charged $10 per lawn. That $10 included the half-an-hour he spent mowing, the time it took to get to the lawn, the price of the gas, the price of maintenance, and the energy Emil spent mowing.

What does Your Competition Charge?

The great thing about having competition is that they've done a lot of the work for you. They've researched the price that customers are willing to pay and the cost of providing the product/service. Their carefully chosen prices are available to customers – and to you.

> Take this book for example. We found a competitor who's charging $97.00 for a guide called *How to Start a Gift Basket Business*. That gave us a hint about what type of price we could charge for this book.

What's the Value to Your Customers?

Every customer is looking for value. The value of your product or service should be greater than or equal to the value of the money that you are asking in return – otherwise, nobody is going to buy it.

The value to your customers is partly determined by the amount of money your product/service will help them save/earn. Ask potential customers how much they would pay for what you offer.

Adam Horwitz sells *Mobile Monopoly* for $37. Why do customers think there is $37 worth of value in it? He demonstrates the value on his sales page, by showing that he used the techniques revealed in *Mobile Monopoly* to earn $51,641.20 in 6 months.

Fine-Tuning with Price Points

Do you ever notice how many prices end in .99 cents? Psychologically, it seems like less money to the consumer.

Online, it has become common practice to end the price of your product in a 7 (the example above, *Mobile Monopoly*, is $37). Try out some different price points and see what works best for your business.

Michael Dunlop recently launched his first product, *Popup Domination*. When he launched, it was $47. He realized that there was more than $47 of value in the product because it helps people make more money. So he upped the price to $77. It must have effected conversions so he recently dropped the price back down to $47.

Your Profitability Day

If you want to know the day that your company will be profitable (based on solid assumptions), use old-school algebra to figure out your break-even point.

1. **Find out how many customers you need.**

   Add up your startup costs and double them. Finalize your price and subtract your costs to determine your profit/unit. Then divide your adjusted startup costs by your profit/unit to figure out how many sales you need to become profitable.

   $$Customers\ Needed\ to\ Hit\ Profit = \frac{2(Startup\ Costs)}{Price - Cost\ per\ Unit}$$

2. **Calculate your profit day.**

   Predict how many customers you can get per month. Now divide the number of sales you need to make by how many customers you think you can get per month. Multiply that number by 30 to figure out how many days it'll take.

$$\boldsymbol{Days\ Until\ Profitable} = \frac{Customers\ Needed\ to\ Hit\ Profit}{Expected\ Customers\ per\ Month} \times 30\ Days$$

Emil Motycka had a profitable business on day one. He borrowed his parents' mower and mowed his aunt's lawn for $10. Three years later, at age 12, he pulled out a four-year, $8,000 loan to get a commercial mower. For two years, every dollar he made went towards paying off that loan because he knew how important it was to have a profitable business.

Most young service-providers charge ½ as much as they should when they're starting out. If you provide a service, you should become profitable in the first week.

4

MARKET YOUR BUSINESS

HONE IN ON YOUR TARGET MARKET

"The best way to attract people is to listen to your customers. What do they want? Once you find that out, then you cater to them."

CATHERINE COOK
Co-Founder of myYearbook

P arty poopers are the worst. When planning your party, only invite your best friends, the people who are fun to be around, and those who are most likely to buy you a present. Start with a list of all your friends and narrow it down to the ones who fit those descriptions.

You need to do the same with your business.

This chapter will show you how to find the best customers and how to build a brand that will get them to do your marketing for you.

SELECT A TARGET MARKET

"I use my age as a marketing advantage. I can target younger people. I say, 'If I'm 18 years old, you could be doing the same thing no matter how old you are.'"

ADAM HORWITZ
Made $1.5 Million in Three Days at 18

Who will give you the most bang for your marketing buck?

Who is Your Ideal Customer?

Ask yourself three questions:

1. **Whose problem can your product or service solve?**
   Start by brainstorming a list of all the organizations or people that your business can help.

2. **Who is most likely to purchase in the largest quantities?**
   From that list, who would be your most profitable customers? And within those organizations, who makes the buying decisions? A small group of very profitable customers is better than a large group of barely profitable customers.

3. **How far can you reach?**

   If you're selling a product, you can sell it and ship it to anyone in the world. But if you're providing a service (that's not digital), you're geographically limited. Either way, it's best to start local and expand later as you prove the validity of your business.

Emil Motycka started mowing residential lawns when he was nine years old. By the time he got to high school, he expanded to commercial properties. He realized that he could make $60/hour in the residential market and only $45/hour in the commercial. So now he markets exclusively towards residential homeowners.

Describe Your Target Market

You need to be able to describe your target market in one sentence.

What's their gender, age, location, hobbies, education-level, family status? What do they eat for lunch? What do they watch on TV? Who are their friends? How do they position their toilet paper?

The more you know about your target market, the more ways you'll find to reach them. If you know that they have BINGO nights on Fridays, you can become a volunteer there.

Emil's target market is middle-to-upper-class, senior citizen homeowners in Northern Colorado because they are more willing to pay and less capable of mowing their lawns and doing the other tasks that Emil's service provides (e.g. aeration, sprinkler installation and repair, landscaping, fall clean-up, sprinkler blowouts, snow removal, etc.).

> Start with a small target market and your business will naturally expand to other markets. When Facebook started it was exclusive to Harvard students. Then they opened it to other Ivy League schools. Then all colleges. Now anyone can get on Facebook.

NARROW DOWN TO A NICHE

"Being a social network in a Facebook and Twitter world isn't easy. You have to really find your niche and use it."

CATHERINE COOK
Co-Founder of myYearbook

Your target market should be no larger than 100 people. Do that by choosing a specific niche. The smaller your niche, the easier it will be to become the best.

People hire the best at what they do.

Start with Target Market

Go back to your one-sentence description of your target market. Use it as a checklist/roadmap to find potential customers.

> When Catherine Cook launched myYearbook she wanted to attract high school students. Marketing to all 19 million high school students in America is impossible. So Catherine started with getting all of her friends at school to sign up. Then she scaled it. Now they make $20 million per year with 22 million members.

Consider People in Your Network

People who know you will be more open to hearing about your business.

Take your broad target market and think of people in your network who fit that description. Approach these people, tell them what you're doing, and get their reaction. You'll definitely get feedback and maybe a customer. It's a two-for.

> Lindsay Manseau has a freelance photography service that specializes in wedding photography. As part of her marketing strategy, she constantly attends networking events with other young adults. Every person she meets is a potential customer.

Networking is her primary method of marketing because that's how the photo biz works.

Find Other People who Fit that Description

Once you've exhausted your network, start finding other people who fit within your target market. This is called generating leads. Ideally, you want to generate leads and have someone within your network to be able to make the introduction to those people.

When we were recruiting our interviewees, we started with a list of young entrepreneurs (leads). Michael Dunlop was one of our first interviewees. Every top young entrepreneur knows Michael. We built our credibility with his name in the emails we sent out to other young entrepreneurs. Michael also introduced us to Stanley Tang and Juliette Brindak.

Cold-calling is much easier when you have a name to drop at the beginning of the conversation. For instance, when someone receives a random phone call, they'll want to know how you got their number. If you have a mutual acquaintance, they'll be more likely to want to hear what you have to say.

NAME YOUR BUSINESS

"A king can do anything when he wants. It's not that I'm going to rule everyone else. It's that I'm going to rule myself… That's what the 'King' means. You can call me Sid. My friends call me Sid."

KING SIDHARTH
19-Year-Old Entrepreneur from India

Starting my company with a bad name is the biggest business mistake I've ever made.

I knew my mission was to help young people start businesses and become entrepreneurs. But I didn't know exactly what age group I wanted to attract. So I got started with the name, "JuniorBiz."

Two years later I realized that the name doesn't appeal to the 20-somethings. "JuniorBiz" implies that the site is meant for kids, not young adults. Now I'm starting over from scratch with the name, "14 Clicks."

Branded vs. Generic

Before you start thinking about names, take a second look at your target market. Only consider names that appeal to that group of people.

- **Branded business name if business-to-consumer (B2C).**
  Branded names like Google, Facebook, and YouTube don't mean anything outside the context of your company. Use a branded name if you're selling to consumers and everyday-people. With a brandable name, consumers are more likely to remember it and you can be more creative in your marketing.

- **Generic business name if business-to-business (B2B).**
  Generic names like Waste Management, General Electric, and International Business Machines (IBM) use the business name to imply what the business does. Use a generic name if you're selling to other businesses and commercial clients. Generic names are intentionally boring because they need to generate an authoritative image to attract other businesses. "Koala Bear Computers" isn't going to garner much respect from a business person even if it is the best option.

Spend more time thinking about your business name if you're B2C. If you're primarily B2B, using the initials of your company founders might be good enough – unless your names are Fred, Allen, Randy, and Tyler.

Emil Motycka has both consumer customers and commercial clients. To appeal to consumers, he's rebranding a portion of his company to "Emil's." To appeal to businesses, he's keeping the generic name at "Motycka Enterprises." Both will be operated under his company name, "Motcyka Enterprises, LLC."

Your Tagline

Your tagline is a catchphrase that you will use to quickly describe your business (no more than 5 words) while capturing people's curiosity.

Like business name, it's important for it to be unique. More often than not, companies trademark their taglines so they're the only business that can use those words in that order.

With 22 million members, myYearbook's tagline is "Friends. Flirts. Fun." That quickly sums up just about everything you can do on myYearbook.com.

Old-school business gurus will tell you that the name doesn't matter. They'll tell you to just get started and let the name come later. With the internet, this is a big mistake. You need to get the domain and start building search engine authority as soon as you can. The name and brand will make or break your company. Just look at Facebook vs. Friendster. What's Friendster? Exactly.

BRAND BASED ON APPEAL

"You're building a brand – and when you have a brand, people just talk about you. That is what you really want."

SYED BALKHI

Founder of WPBeginner and Uzzz Productions

Valued at $70.5 billion, Coca-Cola is the biggest brand in the world. IBM is number two ($64.7 billion). And Microsoft slides into third ($60.9 billion).

Brands are intangible but they're one of the most valuable things you can build for your business.

Your Brand's Message

Start with your message. Based on what your target market likes, what do you want your brand to convey? What do you want someone's first thought to be when they see your logo? The answers to these questions will be the basis of your colors, logo, and tagline.

Catherine Cook wanted myYearbook to be viewed and described as a fun place to meet new people. Everything on her website contributes to representing that message and building that brand.

Psychology of Colors

Colors play a vital role in determining how someone perceives your brand. Here's a list of colors and what they subconsciously represent:

RED	Energy, attracts attention, creates urgency; the first color we see; often used in clearance sales.
ORANGE	Aggressive; creates a call to action: subscribe, buy, or sell.
YELLOW	Optimistic and youthful; often used to grab attention of window shoppers.
GREEN	Associated with wealth; easiest color for the eyes to process; used to relax in stores.
BLUE	Creates sensation of trust and security; often seen with banks and businesses.
PURPLE	Soothing and calming; often seen in beauty or anti-aging products.
PINK	Romantic and feminine; used to market products to women and young girls.
BLACK	Powerful and sleek like me; used to market luxury products.

Blue is the primary color that is used on myYearbook.com. This sets an inviting environment that builds trust with new visitors. All the other colors help to build a friendly and fun feel to their website.

The myYearbook header builds trust and implies fun!

Your Logo

It's the face of your company. You'll put your logo on business cards, marketing materials, websites, and, if your brand is cool enough, people will get it tattooed on their arm. There are three types of logos:

1. **Logotype/wordmark logos represent your brand as a font.** Different types of font portray different meaning and appeal to different types of customers. Script or thin fonts imply formality and appeal to luxury-seekers. Thick fonts convey strength and power. Slanted fonts impart a sense of motion or forward-thinking.

2. **Iconic/symbolic logos are images that portray your brand.** When using an icon or symbol to represent your business, it needs to be particularly simple, recognizable, and memorable. You should be able to describe the shape in a few words, e.g., "swoosh", "golden arches", and "apple".

3. **Combination marks use text and an image (Recommended).** It's the best of both worlds and what you should use. The image attracts visual people and gives people a name to remember you by.

37

Here are five basic principles that make a good logo:

1. **Keep it simple, sweetheart.**
   Simple is easily recognizable and incredibly memorable.

2. **Keep it appropriate to the brand message you want to build.**
   Once again, everything from the colors, to the fonts, to the shapes and the thickness of the type contribute to the brand you want to convey.

3. **Be creative.**
   You want people talking about you. People talk about things that are unique and creative. Your logo is an opportunity to be unique and creative. For instance, has anyone ever told you that there's an arrow in the FedEx logo?

4. **Needs to be scalable.**
   So it can be seen on a skyscraper from but also placed on the corner of a small pamphlet.

5. **Needs to be recognizable in black and white.**
   Always printing in color is expensive. Eventually, your logo will appear in black and white. Make sure people can still recognize it when it does. Don't rely on different colors to make it memorable.

At 22-years-old, Jacob Cass is one of the world's premier logo designers. You bet he has a great logo. It's drawn in and looks like a pencil, which is the first tool he uses to make a new design. Also, J.C.D. are the initials of his company, Just Creative Design. J.C. is his personal initials. See his logo below:

JUST CREATIVE DESIGN

Jacob Cass's logo looks like a pencil.

Where to Get an Affordable Logo

To make a semi-professional logo, the software alone costs $700. Your logo is one of the few things you should outsource when you're starting out (unless you're a designer).

Keep in mind that the logo is the face of your company, the cornerstone of your brand. But I understand that you need to stick to a tight budget. Here are four options for getting a logo, from dirt cheap to top-of-the-line.

1. **Dirt Cheap Logo, $27**
   If you want to spend as little as possible, use LogoNerds. For $27, people will see that at least you didn't make it yourself. They give you three options and guarantee your satisfaction. To get a cheap logo, go to www.LogoNerds.com.

2. **Affordable Logo, $45**
   Next cheapest is LogoInn. For $45, they only give you one logo concept but it's slightly higher quality. They have other options for more concepts. Logoinn also has a 100% satisfaction guarantee. To take a look at Logoinn's options, go to www.LogoInn.com

3. **Professional Logo, $295 (*Recommended*)**
   If you want to guarantee professional quality, use 99designs. It was started by a young entrepreneur and is the fastest growing design service in the world. For a minimum of $295, you submit a project to their site. Within hours dozens of designers submit logos and compete to win your bid. Choose your favorite out of an average of 100 logos and only that designer gets paid. To get a professional logo, go to www.99designs.com.

4. **Really Professional Logo, $1000+**
   Traditionally, when people hired someone to make a logo for them, that process would include sitting down with the designer for an hour or so. This lets them get a grasp of the brand you want to create. Then the designer spends a few

hours perfecting all the colors, lines, type, and mark to hammer down the fundamentals of the logo. Go this process to get the perfect logo, but it's much more expensive than the alternatives. If you want to find and hire an individual designer, go to www.Elance.com.

Michael Dunlop used 99designs to get his new logo made. You can see the old vs. the new below:

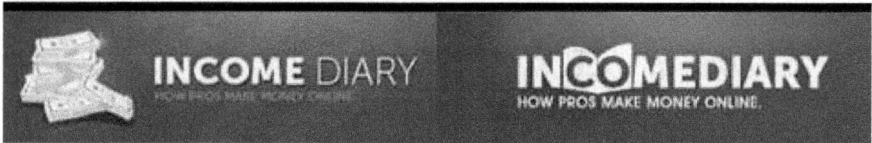

| Old Logo | New Logo |

A good indication of the quality of work you can expect from a design company is their logo. If their logo and web design is sub-par, you're going to pay for a bad logo.

Your T-Shirts

Every company should have t-shirts. You can wear them on the job or give them away to your best customers. Heck, you might even be able to sell them to your customers. People are more likely to wear t-shirts that they buy.

Having t-shirts is one of the few ways you can sell your marketing materials. If you're going to sell them, make sure you're selling something people want to wear and be associated with. That's why you need to build a brand that people like.

One of the first things Ben Weissenstein did when he decided to start his business is go to Walmart and buy two red polos as uniforms. Now, all of his staff wears blue polos with his logo embroidered on them. This gives his business a very professional brand image that his customers want to share with their friends.

Building a solid, likable brand is the most important thing you can do for your business. With a good brand, people will come to you and you'll never have to spend a dime on advertising. This will save you a lot of money and make you famous.

5

REACH YOUR CUSTOMERS

LET PEOPLE KNOW THAT YOU EXIST

"Once we get all the bugs worked out, we're going to hit the market button. By the end of the year, revenue should be $100K per month."

ANDREW FASHION

Made $2.5 Million by 21

W hen I was a kid, I was obsessed with baseball cards. I collected them so I could sell 'em down the road. There's only one problem. I never let anyone know that they were for sale. Now I have a massive inventory of over 6,000 baseball cards.

Now that you have a business, you need to let people know about it. By the end of the chapter, you're going to know the best ways to advertise your business and the golden structure for getting them to buy.

By the way, are you interested in a mint-condition, 1994 Pinnacle Chipper Jones Rookie Card? If so, make an offer.

YOUR NETWORK IS BUSINESS

"I enjoy networking with people. That's how you get further in this business."

SAVANNAH BRITT
World's Youngest Magazine Publisher

If there's one thing that every entrepreneur needs to do, it's network. I'm not talking about filling your quota of one event per month. You need to network daily with almost everyone you meet.

"What do you do?"

I get this question all the time, and I don't like answering it. Either I bore them to death with all the things that I do. Or I summarize a few of my daily tasks, and they just say, "Oh, that's cool. Do you want to know what I do?" My business is my biggest passion and you're not even the slightest bit interested?

As an entrepreneur, there's only one good way to answer this question. It's called an elevator pitch. It's a 60-second summary of the vision you have for your company.

1. **Use the first 20 seconds to hook them with your story.**
   Something about whom you are and why you're passionate about what you're doing. This will add a personal touch to your pitch.

2. **Spend the next 15 seconds to diagnose the problem.**
   What's the problem and how big is it? If you know stats, throw them in.

3. **Run through the next 15 seconds with your solution.**
   Why are you the best in the world at it?

4. **Finish the last 10 seconds with a call-to-action.**
   "What do you think?" "What advice do you have?" "Do you know anyone who can help?"

Because it's only 60 seconds and it's structured to induce curiosity, they'll pay attention. Every time someone asks you what you do, respond with your elevator pitch.

One of the most polished elevator pitches I've ever heard came from Sabirul Islam. Part of it came when I asked him for the single most important reason for his success, he said, "The Three Strikes: the intensity, the integrity, and the intelligence. You need to have the intensity, the strength, to follow your passion. In terms of integrity, you have to be honest with yourself as well. And then the rest is intelligence."

Get to Know Your Neighbors

People in your community could be your first customers. So it's important to get to know them before you try to sell to them.

Always say hi, waive when you drive by, smile when you see them, and ask them how they're doing on a regular basis. Always be neighborly and you'll build a good reputation in your community. Not just in your neighborhood, but in your community as a whole.

Catherine Cook was well-liked while she was in high school because she was nice to everyone. When she launched myYearbook.com in 2006, it spread like wildflowers throughout her school. Now it boasts 22 million members.

Attend Networking Events

One of the most important things you can do when you're first getting started is attend local entrepreneurship events. Meet all the entrepreneurs in your community and build a reputation as someone they all want to help. Once you feel comfortable introducing yourself to strangers; start going to the networking events that your target market attends.

That's where you'll start picking up customers. Your goal at these events is to introduce yourself to lots of people, qualify them in the first few minutes by figuring out if they would be a good customer. If they aren't, move on to the next person. Become someone they like and get their business card. Follow-up with an email the next day to schedule a meeting where you can close the sale. This is best over coffee or lunch. If you pay, they'll feel like they owe you.

To find a local networking event, go to www.Meetup.com.

One of the best things you can do to grow your business is attend national conferences with other people in your field. Your goal with these events is to meet the big shots in your industry. Become friends with them and they'll help you by introducing you to other important people as, "someone worth talking to."

To find a relevant national conference, go to www.Lanyrd.com.

When I got started, one of the first things I did was attend the local Entrepreneurship Meetup. I met the founders and they let me speak about my business to the whole group. Now, the majority of the entrepreneurial community in Fort Collins at least knows about me. I've also gone to two national entrepreneurship conferences where I've become good friends with Syed Balkhi, Michael Dunlop, Andrew Fashion, Marshall Haas, and Adam Horwitz.

Get Free Business Cards

You can't call yourself a business person until you have a business card. Take them everywhere. You'll meet people almost every day who will want to help you. It's your responsibility to give them an easy way to contact you.

Thankfully, Vistaprint will help you get your 250 cards for "free" (just pay shipping).

1. **Go to Vistaprint.com**
   Click "Free Business Cards" on the bottom left of the homepage. In the upper right of this page you'll be able to watch a snazzy video that will walk you through everything.

2. **Front side**
   i.   Company Name – If you have it, include your LLC (e.g. "14 Clicks, LLC").
   ii. Company Message – Your tagline.
   iii. Your Name – Your full name.
   iv. Address – Your position in the company (e.g. "Founder").
   v.   Phone - Your direct line.
   vi. Email - Best to have "...@yourdomain.com". Next best, "...@gmail.com". Create a Gmail account if you don't already have one.
   vii. Website - Leave off the "http://www." (e.g. "14clicks.com").

3. **Select your design**
   Choose the one that most accurately reflects your company. You can also upgrade to a premium design or submit your own. Continue as a guest unless you have an account.

4. **Select your options**
   i. Quantity – Stick with 250 for free.
   ii. Paper Stock – Get matte finish for free. Glossy is the next best option.

    iii.   **Back Side** – The free option includes an advertisement for Vistraprint on the back. I recommend going "Black | No Printing" for a few bucks more.

    iv.   **Matching** - You don't need anything else unless it catches your fancy.

    v.   **Recommended** - You don't need anything here but I've always wanted one of those metal business card holders.

    vi.   **Free Internet Marketing** – Don't do it. They'll buy and own the domain you want and charge you monthly to use it.

5. **Checkout**

Finish filling out the Delivery Address, Billing Address, Payment Information, and print out your Order Confirmation. Your business cards should arrive within 2-3 weeks.

To get free business cards, go to www.Vistaprint.com.

I know they advertise this deal as "free" and you have to pay for shipping, but anything under $15 for business cards is a steal. Some printers charge upwards of $80 – $100 for 250 business cards.

I got my first set of business cards from Vistaprint. I ordered them a few weeks before a big networking event. The week before, they still hadn't arrived. So I contacted customer support and they rush delivered 250 more. Within a month, the first batch came too. So I had 500 business cards and I'm still working through them.

Networking is a process. People do business with their friends. Anytime you meet someone who can help you, start by asking how you can help them. Then, actually help them and they'll find a way to help you.

HOW TO REACH THEM

"I remember last year, I was approaching Matt Groening, the creator of The Simpsons. I was so star-struck that I was shaking, thinking, 'Oh – this guy is a legend!' But you just have to make it happen."

LAUREN AMARANTE
Co-Founder of World Entrepreneurship Day

Reach people how they want to be reached.

Some people hate getting cold-calls while others respect the fact that you'll contact them out of the blue. Figure out how your target market wants to find out about your business. Then do that.

Face-to-Face

If you're selling a big-ticket item, they're going to want to meet you. They're going to want to see your face and judge your character, a lot like a job interview. If you're expecting them to spend over $1,000 with your company, you owe them a free lunch.

This means you need to schedule a meeting. It might even mean that you have to introduce yourself by going to their office or house to schedule that meeting.

Emil Motycka mows lawns for his customers at $20-40 per week. Including his other services, the average customer spends over $1,000 per year with his company. Before he adds on a new customer, he makes a point to meet them in person at their house and give them a personalized quote for their lawn. They sign the contract on the spot.

Phone Call

A phone call is the classic method for reaching out to new customers. It's easy. Get a phone book. Flip to the yellow section where all of your potential customers are grouped together. Go down the list and give each of them a call. In an hour, surely you can set up a few meetings or conference calls.

Keep in mind; you'll probably get a higher conversion rate if you take the time to visit. But making phone calls is much more efficient. If you don't have much luck with phone calls, stop by for a visit.

> Michael Simmons, one of my mentors, started the Extreme Entrepreneurship Tour. When he was first starting out, he racked up $40,000 in debt. To get out of it, he started doing nothing but sales calls. Now he has a staff that does 500 sales calls per day.

Email

If your target market is really busy or spends much of their time on the computer, send them an email. Emailing them is the lesser alternative to a phone call, unless you know that that's how they prefer to be contacted.

Whatever you do, don't template-ize your email. It's obvious when you do. If you value this person as a potential customer, give them the courtesy of a personalized email that you wrote from scratch. Have a similar structure and style in every sales email, but no copy-pasting, at all.

I don't care if it saves you an extra 47 minutes a day. A fake, template-y email is not how you want to start a relationship with a customer. You wouldn't send a template-y email to a bunch of pretty girls asking for a date, would you? I have never done that. Not once.

> When Alex Maroko was struggling to sell his basketball training courses, he started emailing people to see if they wanted to become affiliates. He emailed 60 website owners asking if they wanted to promote his course. Only a handful of them got back to him. With less than ten affiliates, he went on to make $20K the next week.

Direct Mail

Actually mailing your advertising to your target market is expensive. But people with the big budgets narcissistically want you to spend money to be able to get in touch with them. One of my mentors told me that this is how some business owners think.

If you're mailing a post card, pamphlet, or letter, it will cost you about a dollar per mail piece. That doesn't include acquiring the list of people to mail to, which can be a couple grand depending on how targeted you want the list to be.

If you're just starting out, gather your list yourself and be selective to limit your costs. Plus, if you were to mail out to a couple thousand people and got a hundred customers in your first week, that might cripple your company before you even start.

> Emil Motycka has a lawn maintenance company, a commercial cleaning company, a snow removal company, and a recently acquired gardening company. When he sends out his invoices at the end of a season, he includes a 'stuffer' that promotes his other company for the next season (e.g. lawn customers get a snow flier). He gets anywhere from a 20-90% conversion rate depending on the call-to-action.

Flyers

Flyers include everything from door-hangers to three-fold-pamphlets. If you're just starting out and want to sell your service primarily to people in your neighborhood, print up a stack of fliers and go door-to-door. If they answer, shake their hand, ask them how they're doing, and briefly tell them about what you're doing. Then give them a flier with your contact info. If they're not home, hang it on the door.

> When I started my lawn service at age 12, I made a one-page flier and stapled a coupon for 20% off the first mowing. Then I went to every house and introduced myself. Over the six years that I was in business, I mowed about half the lawns in my neighborhood.

Online Job Postings

If you provide a digitally-rendered service like graphic design, web development, or freelance writing; you can easily get customers online. Here are three places where you should create an account to post your portfolio:

1. **Elance**

   Elance is the biggest online job posting site in the world. They're about to eclipse $350 million worth of jobs that they've paid out to freelancers. To post your business for free, go to www.Elance.com.

2. **Freelancer**

   With over $80 million paid out, Freelancer is the next largest job posting website. If you are looking to get more jobs, try posting your portfolio with them as well. To get a free account, go to www.Freelancer.com.

3. **oDesk**

   oDesk is another popular website, but as a freelancer, it's hard to get quality jobs. I've found that oDesk has a lot of service providers who are willing to work for $5-10 per hour. This is great if you're looking for people to do the work for you, but not so good if you're a freelancer. To check it out, go to www.oDesk.com.

These three sites are great for starting your business and getting work under your belt, but these types of jobs can't sustain you for the long-term. Eventually you'll have to find customers on your own then you can hire freelancers from those sites to do the work for you.

Your Website

Most of the advertising methods thus far have been geared towards service-based businesses. That's because most young entrepreneurs sell their products on the internet. It's hard to get a product into retailers, setting up a booth is expensive, and going door-to-door to make a one-time sale is impractical. Leave that to the scouts.

The first thing you need is a website. Make sure you rank for the right keywords and once visitors land on your website, there's a clear call-to-action. That call-to-action can be to fill out a form, give you a call, or purchase your product. Without a fancy, software-y website, blogging is the best way to get consistent traffic.

Social media isn't advertising. Think of your Facebook Page or Twitter Stream as an extension of your website. It's another place for people to interact with you and for you to build friendships. As soon as you start pumping out links to buy, those friends lose respect for you. If you wouldn't say it to a good friend, don't status it or tweet it.

We put together Click 3 to show you how to create an online business. If you want a step-by-step process for creating a website, getting traffic, and making sales, go to www.14clicks.com/click3

Jacob Cass, a graphic designer, has done such an outstanding job developing, designing, and managing his website and social media that he never needs to advertise. He ranks #19 on Google for the highly-competitive term "graphic designer" and he gets more leads than he can fulfill. JustCreativeDesign.com showcases his work, his personality, his achievements, and there's a clear call-to-action. *Hire* him. This lets him charge a minimum of $3,700 for a brand identity and business card design.

If you're selling something big, start with sending them an email or direct mail. Follow-up with a phone call asking them if they received the email/direct mail. If they did, you don't have to make a cold-introduction. If they deleted it or threw it away, they will feel indebted and will at least listen to what you have to say. In your email, direct mail, and phone call, your goal is to set up a face-to-face or virtual meeting to make your sales pitch.

THE GOLDEN SALES PITCH

"People are always, always, always going to have questions and objections about buying things. As they're reading your sales letter or watching your sales video you want to be answering that objection. That's just basic marketing."

ALEX MAROKO
From $0 to $100K in Five Months

This is the golden structure for getting someone to buy something:

1. **Build a relationship.**
   Constant networking, rapport, curiosity.

2. **Empathize with their struggles.**
   Your story, how you're like them, teach them what you know, cultivate credibility.

3. **Demonstrate your solution.**
   Features, advantages, benefits.

4. **Comfort their hesitancies.**
   Coupons, testimonials, guarantees.

5. **Close the sale.**
   Time-sensitive, sense of urgency, make it easy to buy.

Using that structure, here's how you prepare various marketing materials.

Posters, Fliers, and Pamphlets

When you're designing your posters, fliers, and pamphlets, you don't need to include the entire golden structure because the call-to-action is different. You have to be succinct. In most cases, you're trying to get them to call you or visit your website. Not trying to get them to purchase. Your conversation, meeting, or website is where they'll purchase.

There are six essentials of print advertising:

1. **Headline.**
   To attract their attention and gain their curiosity. The headline is always read first. It's sole purpose is to get them to read the next line.

2. **What you're selling.**
   The features, advantages, and benefits to your product or service. Benefits being most important.

3. **Instructions for hiring or buying.**
   The call-to-action. Tell them what to do or they won't do anything. This is also called direct-response marketing because you're asking them to do something as a result of reading the ad.

4. **Your name and/or picture.**
   To add a personal touch to the advertising.

5. **Your business name and/or logo.**
   To add credibility and give them something to rememeber.

6. **Contact information.**
   Your phone number, email, and/or website. Let them choose how to contact you.

If you want to boost the conversions (how often someone does what you want them to do), attach a coupon for a minimum of 20% off that expires within a month. Anything less than 20% seems chincy and the expiration date motivates them to act soon.

Here's an ad that we had in the Fall/Winter 2010 Self-Made Magazine:

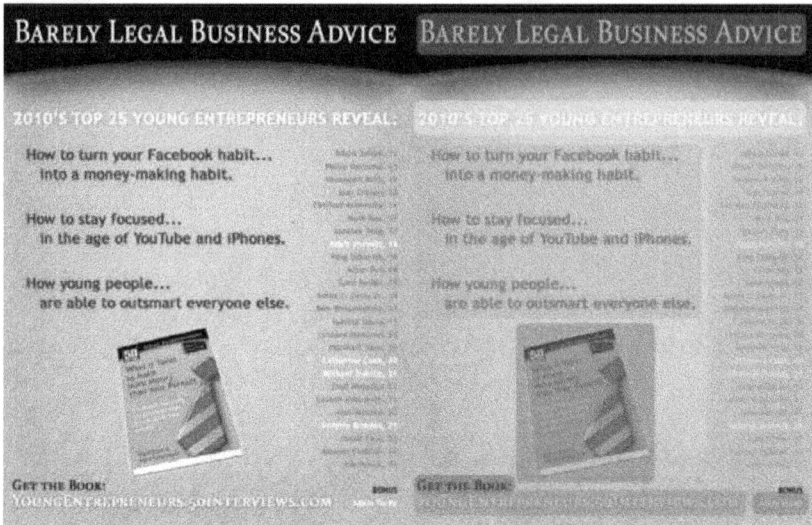

Headline (red) - "Barely Legal Business Advice"

What we're selling: *Features (orange) – Names of interviewees, Advantages (yellow) – "Top 25 Young Entrepreneurs", Benefits (green) – "How to…"*

Instructions for buying (blue) – "Get the Book"

Your name *(purple) – Adam Toren, Self Made Publisher*

Your logo (pink) – Image of book

Contact information (gray) – Our website

> On a one-page flier or poster, always put the headline at the top and the call-to-action or logo in the bottom right. When people consume print ads, they start in the upper left and move to the bottom right. The same applies to websites.

Sales Pitch with Objection Handlers

Personal selling is an art. I'm bad at executing it but I know how it works. Once you set up a meeting with a potential client, here's the process that you need to go through:

1. **Build rapport.**
   This means talking to them about their day, their family, why they love doing what they do, and otherwise getting them to open up and talk to you as a friend.

2. **Ask them about their problems.**
   Once you can tell that they feel comfortable talking to you, ask if you can transition into the presentation. Start by asking if they're familiar with your company. If they say no, give them the gist of who you are, the history of your company, and why you do what you do. Then start asking open-ended questions about their business so you can find the problems that your company can solve.

3. **Tell them about your solutions.**
   Show them how your company can solve their biggest problems and frustrations. Educate them. Teach them something valuable about your solution to show that you know what you're talking about. Start with the attributes or features (what you actually do). Then why you are the best option (advantage over competitors). Then focus and nail down the benefits (what's in it for them). Pull out your sales material and show them the different packages you offer.

4. **Trial close**
   Ask them one of two questions: (1) Do you feel comfortable with everything we've presented thus far? They'll most likely have objections and this is where they'll let you know. If they say yes, move into the close. (2) On a scale of one to ten, ten being most likely, how likely are you to purchase? If less than ten, ask them what objections they have.

5. **Handle their objections.**

   Start by restating their objection as a question. It puts you on the same page, lets them know you were listening, and gets them into the habit of saying yes. Most of the time, they're going to be hesitant about the cost. Here you need to have solid facts and figures to prove how the benefits to your product or service outweigh the costs. Also consider showing them testimonials and giving them a money-back guarantee.

6. **Close.**

   This is when you substantiate why the time to buy is now. Maybe their business is losing money by not having your service. Maybe every day without your product is another day their kids will struggle. Here is where you need to have the contract written up and personalized to them so they can sign on the dotted line.

Did you see how the golden structure was weaved in?

If you can't meet a potential client in person, then you can conduct the same process over the phone, on a conference call, or in a video chat. Skype.com is the best, free way to talk to do a video chat or conference call as long as you both have Skype. Use FreeConferenceCall.com if your client prefers to call-in via phone.

But if you want to be able to talk with someone and show them a presentation that's on your computer, use GoToMeeting. It costs $49 a month, but it'll be much more professional and your potential client can call-in with their phone. Plus, it lets you *demonstrate* your virtual services instead of just talking about them.

To check out it out, go to www.GoToMeeting.com.

Our publisher hosts weekly webinars with his authors to discuss book marketing strategies. He uses GoToMeeting to conduct the webinar because we can login and see his computer. This way he can show us the strategies that he runs through. Our publisher also uses this software to attract new authors.

> To make someone buy, they need to be both logically and emotionally convinced. Get them logically convinced by doing a good job of handling their objections. Convince them emotionally by painting a picture of how their life will improve by hiring or buying from you. "Imagine what it would be like to…"

Sales Copy for Internet

Sales copy for the internet is a little bit different than a face-to-face sales pitch because it's not a conversation. You can't figure out their exact problems so you have to consider all the problems that your product or service solves.

Typically, people think of sales copy for sales pages only. Instead, think of your entire online presence as a sales tool. From blog posts to Facebook statuses, you need to use the sales copy mindset for everything you write.

For the sake of this book, I'll focus on the process of writing a sales page.

1. **Headline.**
   The headline needs to be the first thing they see and the first thing they read. Put it at the top of the webpage and use it to build their curiosity. The goal of a good headline is to make them read the next line. The goal of the first line is to make them read the next line, and so on and so forth, until they've read every line.

2. **Introduce yourself.**
   Who are you? Relate to your target market by detailing the struggles that they're going through (this is the problem you're solving) and how you went through them too. How did you alleviate those struggles? Show them how you did it. If you feel like you're giving up too much information, you're on the right track. How much better is your situation today? The purpose of this section is to build a personal connection with

your visitor while teaching them something to prove your credibility.

3. **Introduce your solution.**
   Start with the components and features of your product or service. What exactly are you offering? Then talk about how and why your solution is better than all of the alternatives. But the main thing you want to focus on is benefits to using your product or hiring your service. Always, always sell benefits. Provide visuals (e.g. picture, digital rendering, book cover image, or an image to symbolize the benefits) throughout this section.

4. **Address every possible objection.**
   Think of every reason they could say no, and give them a reason to say yes. Price is almost always the biggest objection. Offset that by demonstrating the real value (in dollar amounts if you can) of what you're selling. If you let them know about an objection that they didn't think of, it will build trust. Break up your objections with real testimonials from customers to show that other people have purchased it and had a positive experience.

5. **Ask them to buy and make it easy.**
   Put a yellow or orange "Add to Cart" button with blue font at the top and bottom of your sales page. Some people will want to buy it immediately while others will scroll through the copy and reach the end of the page. Psychologically, yellow grabs attention and blue builds trust. Put a blue hyperlink with the anchor text, "Add to Cart" under the button because some people still prefer to click on text rather than images. Also include logos for the different payment methods that you accept (e.g. Visa, Mastercard, PayPal, etc.). This is also where you should tell them about your money-back guarantee.

For *Mobile Monopoly*, Adam Horwitz directed people to a one-page sales page to with nothing but sales copy and a few videos. He started by introducing himself and the struggles he had. Then he calmed every objection throughout the sales page. In the first three days, Adam made $1.5 million. In the following three months, he made another $1.3 million. Below is the actual "Add to Cart" button that Adam used on that sales page:

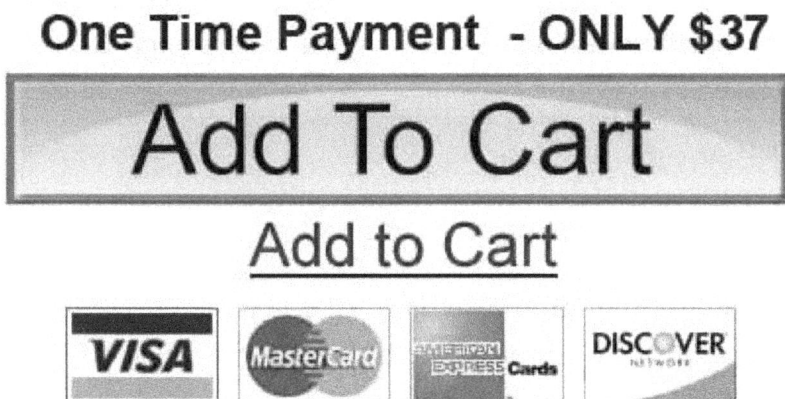

One Time Payment - ONLY $37

Add To Cart

Add to Cart

VISA MasterCard AMERICAN EXPRESS Cards DISCOVER NETWORK

After a few months he knocked down the price from $77 to $37.

One of the most effective ways to increase conversions on your sales page is to have a limited-time offer. But make sure it's a real limited-time offer. If you say you're only accepting three more customers, you better be accepting only three more customers. If I come back a few days later and it still says "Only 3 More Spots, Hurry!", then I've lost all respect for you and I won't be back. Deception might get more purchasers in the short-run, but that's not how you build a long-term brand. If you have an ethical dilemma, ask yourself, "What would Amazon do?"

Sales Video for Internet

People are lazy. The average American spends nine years of their life watching TV.

Good sales pages have sales videos. They let your audience consume your marketing message how they want to consume it. Watching a video is as easy as it gets.

Since video is a more creative medium, the golden structure is more open to innovation. If you can, try to keep the video less than three minutes.

1. **Evoke curiosity.**
   This is your headline. Show them a startling statistic. Pose a peculiar question. Start with the conclusion. Give them a reason to keep watching.

2. **Cultivate credibility.**
   Tell them about how you were once in their shoes. Sitting in that chair. Watching someone else's rags-to-riches, fatty-to-fit, lonely-to-loved story. Then tell them what changed. And show them the results since. Maybe it's the car you drive now. Maybe it's your rockin' bod. Or maybe its pictures from your latest family vacation with the spouse of your dreams. Also, two things that will always generate immediate credibility are logos from press and endorsements from famous people.

3. **Build up the benefits.**
   The whole time you're telling them about how great you life is, you're building them up to the point where you say, "And now I'm going to show you how you too can become _____, _____, and _____."

4. **Expose the problem.**
   But! There's something standing between them and their dreams, and only you can show them how to take it down.

5. **Educate them.**
   Give them a hardy taste of your solution. Just because you can put the Wall Street Journal logo next to your name doesn't mean they respect you, yet. Show them the gist of how they can solve the problem themselves. Give them something they don't know. Once you teach someone something, they become your fan. If you think you're teaching them too much, you're on the right track.

6. **Entice them to take action.**
   Conclude your video with a call-to-action. Maybe it's to buy, opt-in, or watch the next video. Tell them what you want them to do and make it childishly clear. Give them a good reason to do it too. You can't just tell someone to jump off a bridge and expect them to do it. If you tell them that there's a Reese's down there, they're more likely to jump. A million Reese's'? Even more likely. End it with a compelling reason to take action. Use a cliffhanger.

If you want to watch Michael Dunlop's sales video, go to www.PopupDomination.com.

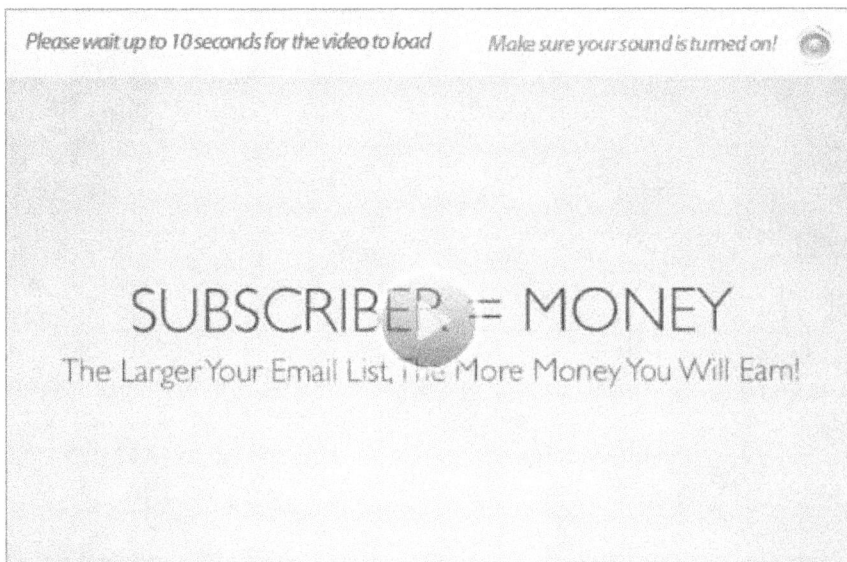

Please wait up to 10 seconds for the video to load   Make sure your sound is turned on!

SUBSCRIBER = MONEY
The Larger Your Email List, The More Money You Will Earn!

He doesn't tell you how long it lasts to keep people engaged.

If you truly have the solution to their problems and you do a good job of communicating the benefits to that solution, they'll be ready to buy before you ask.

6

LIFT OFF

TRANSFORM YOUR PLANS INTO ACTION

"Business is like a rocket ship. It takes a ton of work to get off the ground, but once you get off the ground a little bit, you just start flying."

ALEX MAROKO
From $0 to $100K in Five Months

D o you remember Balloon Boy? You might remember how idiotic his parents were for exploiting their children. But you might not realize how brilliantly they built their pitch for a reality TV show. Everything – from the actual balloon to the media scare to the Falcon puke – was carefully (although recklessly) crafted to get at their goal: to get a TV show.

They haven't accomplished their goal yet but they did get the majority of America to know about their family. If you want the majority of America to know about your business, there are a few respectable ways you can make that more likely.

By the end of the chapter, you'll have a checklist to know if your business is ready for a launch, and how to launch it.

ALL SYSTEMS GO?

"Overnight success doesn't exist. eMillions took 15 months. But, then it seemed like it came out of nowhere when the book launched."

STANLEY TANG
Instant Amazon Best-Seller at 14

Before you launch a bottle rocket, you need a fully-functional bottle rocket, a lighter, and a lookout for the cops.

Before you launch your business, you need a plan to launch it, a process for fulfilling orders, and a system to accept payments.

Why Your Launch Needs to Be Big

Why does your business even need to be launched? Can't we just open up? Yeah, you can just "open" your business. But why? Other than for your own vanity, there are three reasons to plan and execute a launch:

1. **It practically guarantees a customer.**
   One of the biggest challenges for a startup is to acquire the first customer. You're unproven and nothing will deflate your sails more than not getting that first customer. If you're putting some planning and effort into a launch, and couple it with a limited-time coupon, you're bound to get at least one sale.

2. **It creates buzz for your biz.**
   People like to be a part of an event. By making an event out of opening your business, people will be more excited about it. There's a reason you see so many "Grand Opening" signs on new businesses. They leave them up as long as they can because it gets customers excited before they even become a customer. Plus, launching a business gives you a chance to get press, especially if you're young.

3. **People need to see things multiple times before they buy.**
   There's an age-old marketing concept that consumers need to see something seven times before they purchase. That's why big companies advertise everywhere. By launching your business, it increases the likelihood of reaching a potential customer multiple times in a short period of time.

Adam Horwitz did an incredible job of launching *Mobile Monopoly*. He pulled in $1.5 million in the first three days.

Fulfill Orders?

Before you open your doors for business, make sure you can supply the business. You better have a working knowledge of the service you're going to provide or an inventory of the product you're going to supply.

There's a BlackBerry commercial where a business owner's purse gets noticed by a fashion icon. Over the course of the next 30 seconds, he receives a half-million unexpected sales and the guy throws his arms in the air for victory. Outside of commercial-world, a fledgling entrepreneur would not be in a position to fulfill an extra 500,000 orders. That would cripple a real business.

Accept Payments?

How many ways do you accept money? Cash-only doesn't cut it. Even cashing checks requires a bank account. And you'll be losing money if you don't accept credit cards.

Traditionally, to accept credit cards you needed to pay for a merchant account. Those run upwards of $200 per year, and that's just the annual feel. Today, there are a number of options to accept credit cards for minimal fees.

- **PayPal Invoicing**
  You can get their email, give them the product or service, and send them an email invoice later. To get a free account, go to www.PayPal.com.

- **Square (Recommended)**
  Twitter co-founder, Jack Dorsey, founded a new company that lets you accept credit card payments everywhere. Download their app, register your account, apply to accept payments (need bank account number, social security number, and mailing address), and they'll send you a free credit card reader that you plug into the audio jack on your Smartphone. When you accept a payment, your customer automatically receives an email receipt. To get a free Square, go to www.SquareUp.com.

If you have an online ordering system, test it. Then test it again. Go through the same process that you want your customers to go through. To accept payments online, here are a few of the good options:

- **PayPal**
  PayPal is the industry standard for bootstrapping' entrepreneurs. The checkout system works great but it requires your visitors to leave your site to make the payment. If

you want them to stay on your site, you need a PayPal Website Payments Pro account that costs $30 per month and requires some coding. To get a free account, go to www.PayPal.com.

- **ClickBank**
  If you have a digital product and would like to recruit people to help you sell it in exchange for a commission, use ClickBank. They're the biggest affiliate network and marketplace in the world. However, a lot of spammy internet marketers sell with ClickBank, which has given them a bad reputation. Otherwise, it's a highly-reputable company. To take a look, go to www.ClickBank.com.

- **Shopify (Recommended)**
  Shopify is an easy way to create an online store and accept credit card payments. It requires people to purchase through Shopify's site, but you can customize and brand everything from the store to the checkout line. To check out Shopify, go to www.Shopify.com.

- **WP e-Commerce (Recommended if WordPress)**
  If you have a WordPress site, use WP e-Commerce as your shopping cart. It's a free, highly customizable plugin that's easy to set up and it lets you keep the shopping process on your site. To check out WP e-Commerce, go to www.GetShopped.org.

Note: If you want to learn how to create and optimize a WordPress website for your business, check out www.14clicks.com/click3.

Adam used ClickBank to process orders for *Mobile Monopoly*. The reason he was so successful is because he had affiliates send millions of emails out to their lists promoting his product. ClickBank handled all the orders and processed all of the affiliate commissions. He just sat back and watched the money roll in.

> Most online shopping carts have a feature where you can do a test purchase. This way you don't lose your 64 cents to the transaction fee. Also, if you have a fragile product, ship it to yourself to see if it arrives intact.

OFFLINE LAUNCH

"The best thing that you can do is to launch your product. Don't just put it out there."

ALEX MAROKO
From $0 to $100K in Five Months

Imagine if no one made a big deal about your birth. If you hear your parents talk about the day you were born as 'just-another-day-in-between-breakfast-and-dinner'.

Give your business a birth and make it celebratory.

Distributing Flyers

Going door-to-door handing out fliers is the classic way to launch a neighborhood-based business. If you want to start a lawn service, babysitting business, or any service that everyone needs, this is the way to go.

By door-to-door, I mean ring the doorbell, shake their hand, and present the flier with both hands. Treat the flyer as something they should prize.

Also, feel free to attach a small gift or coupon to the flier. For instance, in the spring you can staple a pack of flower seeds. They probably won't use them, but they won't easily forget about it either.

I kicked off my second year of mowing lawns by distributing fliers. I made sure everyone knew I was available for weekly mowing or vacation mowing. I made a couple grand that summer. Not bad for a 13-year-old.

Press Release to Newspapers

If you're a young entrepreneur, one of your advantages is that it's easier to get press about your business. A young person launching a business is newsworthy. People like to read about these prodigy kids so journalists like to cover them.

One way to practically guarantee press is through a press release. In the press release, make sure you identify the hook (why people going to find you interesting), answer why now is the time (make an event out of launching your business), and give them an easy way to contact you.

Then send it to your local newspapers and magazines as a PDF file. On their website they will have an email listed to receive press releases. If you think your business is newsworthy on a national level, send it through a newswire like PRWeb.com and you never know who will pick it up.

Catherine Cook received about 25 major press mentions (e.g. TechCrunch, Mashable, Yahoo!, Fast Company, etc.) in 2010 for myYearbook.com. When something major is going on with their company, they post press releases to their website. As a 20-year-old running a $20 million business, she is exceptionally newsworthy and this has contributed greatly to spreading awareness for her business.

Partnering with Complementary Businesses

Another way to get clients that most entrepreneurs don't know about is partnering with complementary businesses to get referrals or contracts.

If you're running a photography service, get in touch with all of the bakeries in town and ask them to refer their wedding cake customers to your wedding photography service. If other businesses consistently send customers your way, thank them with gift cards or offer free services.

You can also get in touch with larger businesses and ask to become an independent contractor. As a sub-contractor, they hire you to provide a service that they're contracted to provide. You're an independent employee that operates as a freelance business. This is an easy way to get your business up and running.

Emil Motycka runs a lawn maintenance business in northern Colorado. In the winter, he has a snow removal service with large commercial contracts. When there's a big snowstorm, he can't possibly fulfill all of the contracts at the same time. So he has a network of about 65 people that he contacts and trusts that they'll provide the service in the areas he can't. Then he invoices the customer and pays the sub-contractors about 80% of the contract, keeping the other 20% as his referral fee.

Collecting Leads and Making Calls

If you're going to be offering a product or service over $500, then you should meet your customer face-to-face (or at least talk to them). This means you need to collect a list of people to call, make those calls, and try to set up a sales meeting.

A phone book is a great place to start collecting leads. Once you've exhausted those, go through the phone books and directories for your neighboring communities. Then find creative ways to access contact information for potential clients (e.g. local magazines, industry networking events, etc.). Never pay for a list of leads.

The initial sales call is called prospecting. Prospecting calls should last a maximum of five minutes. Your only goal is to schedule a time (20 minutes to an hour) where you can meet with them and pitch your business. Again, try to meet for lunch or coffee, somewhere where you can purchase something for them. A $4 coffee is well worth a $500 contract.

Eventually, you're going to want leads to come to you and a website is a great way to do that.

Since Emil Motycka has been running his business for 13 years, he no longer has to collect leads. Potential clients come to him through existing customers, Craigslist ads, and his network of websites. He even had to shut down one his sites because he was getting too many leads. But he still makes an effort to call and meet with every new client. This is time-consuming but it's one of the main reasons he has so many loyal clients year-to-year.

Grand Opening Fiesta

You don't need to have a party to celebrate the launch of your business, but it's a good excuse to have some friends over. If you do host some sort of gathering, take plenty of pictures and upload them to your Facebook page, Twitter stream, Flickr account, and website.

When Andrew Fashion launched his social networking site, beModel, he invited hundreds of friends and people from the modeling industry to join him for a private party at a club in downtown Denver. He printed up a backdrop with the beModel logo, set it up at the front of the club, and had models get photographed in front of it all night. Then people uploaded them to Facebook and everyone was asking about it. It was a great way to celebrate and raise awareness for beModel from a grassroots level.

Andrew Fashion in front of the beModel backdrop.

> If you're offering a service, you need business cards. Consider making business cards out of magnets. That way people can put it on their fridge and give you a call when they need your services. Staple these to your fliers and hand them out at networking events. To get cheap magnet business cards, go to www.Vistaprint.com.

ONLINE LAUNCH

"I got featured on the front page of the second largest newspaper in Hong Kong. I think I got something like 15,000 unique visitors in 24 hours. It actually crashed on the day I was featured."

STANLEY TANG
Instant Amazon Best-Seller at 14

When a big website launches, you hear about it. One of the reasons they become a big website, is because they launched it. They told people about it who told people about it. And eventually you heard about it.

Launch your website with the mindset that it's going to be big.

Launch a Website for Your Service

Having a website for a service-based business serves two purposes. (1) It acts as a marketing tool to attract new clients. (2) It provides more information about your business for existing clients. When you make the website for your service, keep those two things in mind.

1. **Create a website.**
   The first thing you need is a domain, hosting, and WordPress. When choosing your domain, keep in mind that keywords are the most important thing to have (unless you aim to build a nationally-recognized brand out of your service). This means that if you're servicing your town, include the name of your

town in the domain (e.g. BoulderMowing.com). But what if you want to expand outside of your town? Then get another name and set up another website for that niche. To Google, the keywords in your domain are the most important keywords. Use WordPress because it is the undisputed champion of content management systems (which allows you to update your site without knowing how to code). You can get your domain, hosting, and WordPress at HostGator. Use our coupon code, **14clicksNick**, to save 25% on hosting. To get cheap hosting, go to www.HostGator.com and use our coupon.

2. **Grab a slick design.**
   Once you've installed WordPress, you need to add a theme to make it look good. There are plenty of free themes out there, but www.WooThemes.com has the best. If you want a theme that's more robust (easily customizable, better for search engines, better looking, etc.), it's worth spending a little bit of money on a premium WordPress theme.
   i.   Beginners – we recommend www.ElegantThemes.com.
   ii.   Intermediate – we recommend www.StudioPress.com.
   iii. Advanced – we recommend www.DIYthemes.com (what we use).

3. **Write About, Services, Portfolio, and Contact pages.**
   Besides your homepage, the four most important pages for your service are the about page, services offered page, portfolio page, and contact page. Your about page is an opportunity to introduce your business, yourself, and build credibility with a potential client. The services page will be where you list all of the services you provide. Include your prices if you have a strict pricing policy. Otherwise, don't include prices because they should vary per project. Then create a portfolio page that has examples of your work. If you provide a digital service, this will be much easier. Remember, the purpose of your site is to collect leads, so you need to have a contact page where they can get in touch with you or

request a quote. You should also put a contact form in the sidebar or a link at the bottom of all the other pages leading to your contact page. This will funnel them into taking action.

4. **Set up an information capturing form.**
A form will allow your visitors to contact you without having to leave your website. This makes it a lot more likely that they contact you. Put a contact form on your contact page by using the Contact Form 7 plugin for WordPress. It works great and is highly customizable. If you intend to blog for your business (which is the best way to get traffic), then use Feedburner.com to let people subscribe by email. This will send them an automated email when you publish a new blog post. If you want to build a list of prospects and customers that you can contact anytime, use Aweber.com, MailChimp.com, or iContact.com.

5. **Create your homepage.**
When you have all the supplementary pages set up, it's time to create your homepage. Keep it simple. You can have a static page where the homepage doesn't change or you can keep the blog as the homepage. For a service, it's best to have a static page that directs visitors to look at your services, check out your portfolio, or contact you.

6. **Regularly update it with new content.**
Publish blog posts every week so visitors have a reason to return to your site. Also. Google gives higher preference to websites that are constantly being updated. It's a lot of work to regularly update your blog. So it might not be worth the extra work until you have a sturdy customer-base and solid systems for providing your service.

There's not much benefit to launching a website for a service-based business because tons of traffic isn't what you want or need.

You need targeted traffic that fills out your form before they leave. Put more effort into search engine optimization so you come up at the top for everything your potential clients will search for if they're looking for a business like yours.

You can easily run a successful service-based website on less than 100 visitors per month if you focus on converting those visitors into customers.

Jacob Cass launched JustCreativeDesign.com for his graphic design freelance business in 2007. Now it has become one of the web's leading resources for graphic designers. In 2010, it received 2.2 million unique visitors and 331,000 of those people looked at his portfolio.

Launch a Product Online

One of the biggest advantages of selling a product over providing a service is that your customer-base is worldwide. But if you don't put effort into launching your website, then your product isn't going anywhere.

If you can afford to provide a commission to people who want to promote your products, launch your product with affiliates in mind. Here's a process to launch your product(s) online with or without affiliates.

1. **Create a website.**
   Just like launching your service, your first step is to create the site. You still need an about and a contact page. If you're accepting payments, technically you should have an earnings disclaimer and a privacy policy.

   Affiliates? A traditional product launch website starts with a squeeze page as the homepage. The goal of a squeeze page is to get visitors to fill out a form with their name and email. They're effective at collecting information but the standard squeeze page with the red headline and highlighted text is getting a bad rep from spammy internet marketers. Once you have their email, you can put them into your auto-responder email series that is designed to eventually get them to take action.

2. **Set up order processing system.**
Once you have the basic website developed, you need a way to accept payments and fulfill orders. Use Shopify.com or GetShopped.org (if WordPress) to create the ecommerce portion of your site. By using a third-party shopping cart to accept payments, you aren't responsible for securing your customers' credit card information.

Affiliates? In order to give commissions to the affiliates who send traffic to your site, use ClickBank.com as your order processing system. All you have to do is put your products on ClickBank then put an "Add to Cart" button on your site that links back to purchase it on ClickBank. This service automatically tracks the traffic that's sent to your site and they pay the affiliates directly out of the revenue from the sale. So you don't have to track anything. Plus, ClickBank has the largest community of affiliates in the world to promote your products.

3. **Make sales page(s).**
If you're selling lots of different products on your site, then your sales pages should be short and simple. Have an image of the product, a description including the benefits, an easy-to-find "Add to Cart" button, a customer review, and anything else that you want to include to motivate them to purchase. Then make sure all of your sales pages have the same format. Do what Amazon does.

Affiliates? Generally, products sold through affiliates have longer sales pages. They start with an attention-grabbing headline that raises curiosity through a benefit of the product. Then they include information about who you are to demonstrate your credibility. Have a video to describe the product and why they should buy it. To maximize the effectiveness of your sales page include testimonials (video testimonials are best), an "Add to Cart" button at the top and bottom, bonuses, and a limited time offer.

4. **Reach out to Press, Bloggers, and Affiliates.**
   Once you have the infrastructure in place, it's time to plan your traffic. Press and blogs are a great source of initial traffic for your website. Make a press release and send it to local and relevant national press. Then start contacting influential bloggers and either offer them a guest post or an interview. They can interview you via email or phone, but they're more likely to accept an email interview because it's less work for them. Also ask them to hold off on publishing your news story, guest post, or interview until your launch date.

   Affiliates? Your goal with recruiting affiliates is to get them to agree to promote your product on your launch day. If you get enough affiliates promoting your product at the same time, some of the people on their lists will receive multiple emails about your product. The fact that multiple people are recommending your product gives you credibility. In addition to recruiting them, you need to have a page on your site with advertising banners, emails, tweets, and other promotional material for them to use.

5. **Schedule launch with a 1-week sale.**
   The final element to launching your product online is to couple the launch with a limited-time sale. This motivates people to take action which will increase the conversion rate from visitors to customers.

   Affiliates? By scheduling your launch, it gives affiliates a pre-determined day that they should send an email out to their lists. By giving them a deadline, they're a lot more likely to follow through.

Three months after his launch, Adam Horwitz still gets 50,000+ visitors a day (1.5 million visits/month) to *Mobile Monopoly*.

Launch a Blog

Launching a blog is different than launching a site for your service or product because you need a lot of traffic to make a substantial income. Since you need so much traffic, you'll have to spend more time in the planning and concept phase to launch it right.

Making money from a blog takes time. Be patient.

1. **Flesh out your concept and site plan.**
   What is the purpose of the site? What niche do you want to write about? Are you qualified to write about this niche? Who is your perfect visitor? How will the blog be organized? How are you going to monetize it? At what point will you quit if it doesn't go as planned?

2. **Create a website.**
   Once you know who the site will be for (hint: it's not for you), choose a domain name that you can build a brand around. Set up hosting and install WordPress.

3. **Grab a slick design.**
   Blog design is becoming increasingly important as more and more people start making websites. It needs to be different and memorable. Choose the right colors and get a good logo for the header. You also need to think about the UI (user interface) and UX (user experience). Is it easy and intuitive to navigate? Does every design element work towards the purpose of the site? Getting a premium theme is good but having a custom theme is better.

4. **Set up a conversion form.**
   Provide a way for them to give you their email address in exchange for getting free, regular updates. One option is Feedburner.com. Another is a paid email marketing program like Aweber.com. The benefit to going the paid route is that

you get access to their email so you can email them anytime, not just when you update your site. When they give you their email they become a subscriber. Subscribers will become regular visitors. Regular visitors become customers.

5. **Solidify content strategy.**
Make a list of all the categories that your articles will fall under. These will become your "Categories." Choose a posting frequency (how often and what days) that you can keep up with. Post at least once a week if you want your blog to become the main source of revenue. Pick the days and times that you post based on when your target audience checks their email.

6. **Soft launch.**
Your first post should be, "What is this website and why am I writing about this topic?" These are the first two questions people have when they visit a new site. Write the first 10-20 articles and auto-post them over the next month or so. The soft launch phase will be during the first 5-10 articles. Use this time to get feedback from friends and family while troubleshooting your site and fine-tuning the design. Don't show anyone the site until you've posted at least five articles. Then start with showing your friends and anyone who might be interested in your topic.

7. **Big launch.**
Once you reach a critical mass of 20 articles, start asking people to spread them across social networks. If you get a lot of traffic before you have 20 articles, there isn't enough content to make people stick. During the big launch phase, start submitting your site to directories, news sites, and guest posting on other blogs in your niche.

8. **Carry launch momentum.**
Prolong the launch excitement as long as you can by settling into your posting routine and constantly providing valuable

content. Ideally, a good percentage of your initial traffic will become subscribers and will continue to visit your site as you update it.

Syed Balkhi launched WPBeginner.com on July 4th, 2009. In the first two months, it received 175,533 unique visitors and 490,644 pageviews. There are three main reasons it did so well. (1) He spent almost a year planning it. (2) He wrote 71 articles in the first two months. (3) A lot of these articles were list posts that went viral on Twitter, StumbleUpon, and three times on Digg.

No matter what type of business you have, it's important to at least know the basics of building a website. This way you can communicate with web developers and internet marketers who build and market your websites. The best way to learn the basics is to build a simple website yourself.

If you want to learn more about how to craft a WordPress website that gets traffic and makes money, check out www.14clicks.com/click3.

GET IT DONE

MASTER THE DAY-TO-DAY

*"I've had it in my mind from a
young age that there's nothing
out there that I couldn't have
if I worked hard enough
to get it."*

KEITH J. DAVIS JR.
19-Year-Old Speaker, Actor, Model, and Author

F or those who don't hail from the south, "Git-r-done" is a commonly used phrase that translates to, "Get the job done."

When it comes to running your business, success is a matter of "gitting-r-done." There are a lot of distractions and easily missed deadlines when you're your own boss. If you make a habit of it, everyday disruptions will be detrimental to your business.

By the end of the chapter, you'll know the best ways to stay focused and productive on what matters most in the day-to-day operations of your business.

YEARLY GOALS → DAILY TASKS

"On top of my bed, whenever I went to sleep, I'd read my goal. It was to make a million dollars by 21.
I may have to update my goal, though.
I set it when I was 15."

ADAM HORWITZ
Made $1.5 Million in Three Days at 18

I ran cross country in high school.

Before every race, I knew that I wanted to finish in a reasonable time. My goal was to run the 5K in under 20 minutes.

Once I knew what I wanted, I figured out that my mile splits had to be between 6:15 and 6:30. This let me pace myself and make adjustments mid-race.

If you want to make progress and stay ahead of the competition, treat your business like a race.

How to Set Goals

Start with your goals. What do you want to do and when do you want to do it by?

Goals need to be Specific, Measurable, Achievable, Relevant, and Time-Bound (SMART) in order to keep you accountable. What exactly do you need to do? How can it be measured? Is it achievable? Is it relevant to your business? And what are your deadlines?

If you're struggling to come up with goals for your business, here are a few questions to elicit starter goals:

1. What day are you going to launch?

2. How much money do you want to make in the first year?

3. How many customers do you need to acquire to make that much money in your first year?

4. How many customers do you need to add per month, week, and day to keep pace?

5. How much money do you want to put back into your business after the first year?

> Before I started 14 Clicks I made nine achievable goals for 2011: 50,000 unique visitors/month, 100,000 pageviews/month, 150 posts, 3,000 comments, 1,000 Facebook fans, 1,000 subscribers, and 100 unit sales of Click 3. I typed them up and printed them out.

Work Backwards from Your Goals

You should have one-year goals, six-month goals, three-month goals, and one-month goals for your business. Start with setting your one-year goals and break those down until you have one-month goals.

> When Syed Balkhi started WPBeginner.com, he set specific six-month goals for the site. He outperformed most of those goals. Once he got to the six-month mark, he re-evaluated his business

and set new six-month goals. Less than two years in, Syed has a top 7,000 website (Alexa).

What Needs to be Done By When?

Use your goals to create deadlines.

Break your goals into individual projects. Then list tasks that need to be completed to finish those projects. Set reasonable deadlines for each task so you can make a to-do list for every day.

Stanley Tang emails his to-do lists to himself so he can access them from anywhere in the world. This helped him stay on task and become an instant Amazon Best-Seller at 14 years old.

Assign Tasks by Urgency & Importance

Once you have a list of everything that needs to git-done, organize daily tasks based on urgency and importance. Some tasks need to be done before you can start others. Other tasks are simply a waste of time.

Make an urgency-importance matrix (2x2) with "Important, Less Important" along the top and "Urgent, Less Urgent" along the left. Go through your list and put each task in one of the quadrants.

	Important	Less Important
Urgent	Eat breakfast Phone calls	Drink coffee Plan day
Less Urgent	Eat lunch Emails	Eat donut Facebook

Go through this process on a regular basis. I do it at the beginning of every week, then work my way through the tasks starting with the Urgent/Important quadrant.

To figure out if a task is worth your time, ask yourself, "Is this task necessary for my business to make money?" Focus your time and effort on the MMA's (Money-Making Activities). If it doesn't lead to you making money, then it's probably not worth your time.

On the other hand, I'm a big proponent of business development. There's a lot of unpaid behind-the-scenes work that you need to do and systems you need to set up for your business to grow. However, MMA's almost always take precedent.

Below is a picture of my Urgency-Importance Matrix for this week as I write this book. You'll see that I used a whiteboard and color-coded the tasks to the various projects that I'm working on. The green project (writing this book) is the most urgent and important.

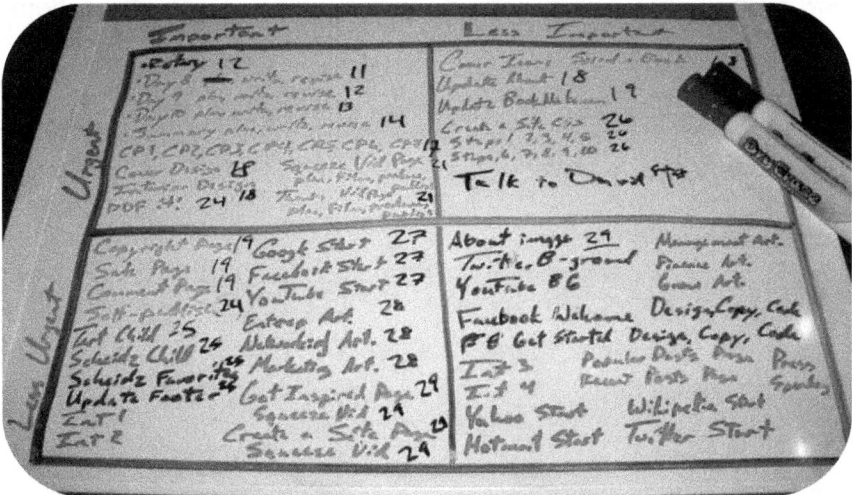

My Urgency-Importance Matrix for the week of January 9th, 2011.

Don't let plans get in the way of best possible course of action. If you're running a race and you feel especially fast, don't be afraid to up the pace.

BE PRODUCTIVE WITH SCHEDULE

"It's a great feeling when you can wake up and say, 'Oh wow – I just made $600 while I was sleeping. I was a productive sleeper!'"

SYED BALKHI

Founder of WPBeginner and Uzzz Productions

I was recently contacted by a guy from California who wanted to meet with me. He was planning a trip to Colorado so we scheduled a dinner.

I didn't write it down because surely I wouldn't forget about it...I did. I felt horrible. I offered to buy him dinner later in the week but he was booked for the rest of his trip. Haven't heard from him since.

Missing a meeting is one of the worst feelings. Here are a few ways to be more productive and to keep track of your day-to-day operations.

11 Productivity Tips

One of the easiest ways to be more successful is to get more done with the time that you have.

1. **Wake up early.**
   In 2007, Yahoo! did a study on 20 CEOs and high-powered executives. One thing they all had in common is that they woke up before 6am. They said it was critical to having a productive day.

2. **Eat well.**
   Countless studies and the age-old adage, "you are what you eat" have proven that a healthy diet leads to a better, more fruitful life. Yet, most of us still opt for fast food or no food at all.

3. **Exercise daily.**

   Like eating well, exercising leads to a healthier life. When you're healthy, your body is able to function at a more efficient level.

4. **Shower and dress nicely even if you're working from home.**

   In high school, my baseball coach bought the entire team new uniforms with his own money. He was convinced that you play better when you look good. Similarly, you are more productive and you talk more eloquently when you're dressed as a professional.

5. **Work in a work-conducive environment.**

   In college, I drove back to campus after dinner to do my homework. The business school created an atmosphere that was designed and engineered to help people be more productive. The extra 20 minutes and $1 of gas was worth being able to reach super-human levels of productivity.

6. **Work with other hard-working people.**

   Another reason I liked to work at the business school was because it was full of other business majors. I wasn't distracted by roommates who wanted to eat cookies and watch movies.

7. **Turn off your phone.**

   According to a Neilson study in 2010, the average 18-24-year-old sends 1,630 texts per month. That's one text every 17 minutes. Turn off your phone. Try it for a day.

8. **Check and respond to email once a day.**

   When you're working on your computer, it's easy to check your email 10-20 times per day. It feels like you're being productive, but you're not. Designate a daily email time and respond to all of your emails then. I like to check email in the morning to see if there's anything urgent. If not, I'll go through and respond at night.

9. **Close unnecessary tabs.**
While on your computer, it's easy to get distracted by lots of open programs and tabs. Close everything that isn't necessary to the task you're performing.

10. **Clock in and out.**
Before you start working, "clock in." This can be as easy as writing down the time, using Online-Stopwatch.com, or tracking your time with FreshBooks. While you're "on the clock" you'll feel like you're stealing company time if you're not being productive. To track your hours with a free FreshBooks account, go to www.FreshBooks.com.

11. **Use RescueTime to monitor your computer productivity.**
RescueTime is one of the niftiest productivity tools on the internet. Install their free software and it automatically tracks and analyzes how you spend time on your computer. They also show you how you compare to other people. To get a free RescueTime account, go to www.RescueTime.com.

According to my RescueTime, I have a .76 efficiency rating and Facebook is my biggest distraction. Three months ago, I spent 4 hours and 53 minutes on Facebook in one week. Last week, that number was down to 2 hours and 11 minutes.

Get a Planner

Keep track of your daily to-do list in a planner. This way, you can open it up in the morning and know exactly what you have to get done that day. If it's in the planner, don't sleep until it's done.

It's like having a boss, accept without the boring stories from his monthly vacations.

Alex Maroko spent $100 on a leather day planner for two reasons. (1) By investing in a planner, he knew he was more likely to use it. (2) So he could tell people about his $100 planner.

Google Calendar

If you're tech-savvy, use Google Calendar to keep track of your schedule. Knowing Google, it has plenty of handy functions like the ability to share your calendar with other people and automatically schedule events from your emails.

I prefer to write things down.

Alex Fraiser, the world's top 17-year-old blogger, has a giant whiteboard to plan and keep track of everything he does. He's one of the most tech-savvy teenagers in the world but he still does his to-dos the old fashioned way, writin' 'em down and crossin' 'em off.

Carry a Notebook Everywhere

Bring a notebook, notepad, or something to write on everywhere you go. You never know where inspiration will strike and it's best to write it down. By designating an entire notebook to these miscellaneous business thoughts, you'll have them all in one place.

Rarely do I leave the house without my keys, phone, wallet, pen, and notebook. I started collecting my business ideas in a 70-page spiral notebook two years ago. Since, I've filled three of them.

The day before a scheduled meeting, send an email to the person you're meeting with the time and date in the subject line. Include the Google Map link for the location of your meeting in the body. This will make it easy to reference and they'll be able to map it with one click.

COMMUNICATE & COLLABORATE

"Younger people can see what's going to happen and what needs to happen. So, I think a lot of older people actually like the fact that I'm young. Lately, they seem to believe everything I say."

ANDREW FASHION
Made $2.5 Million by 21

Also according to Andrew Fashion, when you get a girl's phone number, you should wait five to nine days to call her. It builds anticipation and calling any sooner will make you seem needy.

It's not the same with customers. You need to follow-up as quickly as you can. Unlike girls, customers should be placed on a pedestal.

Here are a few ways to follow-up efficiently and effectively without breaking your productivity.

Schedule Time Daily for Communicating

Make your phone calls in the morning, send your emails at night, and limit Facebook to once a day.

By scheduling your phone calls first thing in the morning, people are more likely to pick up. That's when they're communicating. Also, it sends the impression that you're a professional, not some lazy 20-something who gets up at noon.

Dedicate the heart of your day to the tasks that run the heart of your business.

Then finish up your day with email. This way you can reply to all the people who emailed you throughout the day. Same-day replies show professionalism. By waiting until the end of the day, you don't fall into the endless email cycle of constant replies.

Try to limit both communication times to an hour apiece. This leaves six-ten straight hours for productive work.

When Syed Balkhi is on his computer, he sets his Skype status to *Invisible*. This way he isn't constantly interrupted by his raving fans.

Skype Instant Messaging and Video Calling

Skype is free software that lets you instant message and audio/video chat with your friends. It's becoming the industry standard for communication amongst entrepreneurs.

To register a Skype account and download the software, go to www.Skype.com. Then add me (w.nick.tart) and say, "What's up, Cap'n?" so I know how you found me.

We conducted 21 of the 25 interviews with young entrepreneurs through Skype. Now I can easily chat with them while they're online.

Google Voice Phone Number

If you need to manage a lot of phone calls, get a free Google Voice phone number.

Google Voice gives you one number that clients can call and it redirects to all of your phones. Plus, it transcribes your voicemails and sends them as a text. The coolest feature, however, is that it lets you create personalized voicemail messages for your clients.

Google Voice has plenty of other features, but those three are the best.

The odds of getting the phone number you want will never be more in your favor than they are right now.

A good friend of mine, Trevor Trout, is a salesman for a large company. He has all of his clients contact him through Google Voice. He records a personalized voicemail for each of them. It's a great way to make an impression on new and existing customers.

YouTube Videos

If you charge more than $1,000 for your product or service, consider making personalized videos for prospective clients. Upload them to your YouTube channel and set it to private. Then email the prospective client and include the link to the private YouTube video.

To make the video, get a cheap webcam. YouTube let's you record and upload the videos in one step with a webcam. If you want to be able to show potential clients something on your computer (e.g. all the mistakes with their existing website), use Camtasia to record your screen.

To check out Camtasia, go to www.TechSmith.com/camtasia.

A personalized video is a great way to showcase your skill set and personality as an entrepreneur. But it might not be worth your time unless you're selling something for more than $1,000.

To get a free YouTube channel, go to www.YouTube.com.

> A young entrepreneur named Michal Birecki gave me this tip. He does this and his clients love it. Plus, it gives him in-front-of-the-camera experience for when he's famous.

FreshBooks Project Management

If you're looking to seriously organize your business, use FreshBooks.com. With over two million users, it's one the most widely used project management tools on the internet.

FreshBooks allows you to organize projects, track time, manage team members, track expenses, invoice clients, and run reports. The best part is that you can let clients login to their projects so they can see and pay their invoices online.

They only start charging for this service when you have more than three clients. At that point, you can afford it. To get a free FreshBooks account, go to www.FreshBooks.com.

On the side, I run a freelance web development and marketing service. Before I start working for a client, I create a project for them with FreshBooks. Then they can login and see what I'm doing, when I'm doing it, and how long it took. That way they know exactly what they're paying for.

> The more valuable the customer, the richer the channel of communication needs to be. If you're selling $2 bracelets, you shouldn't need to talk to all of your customers. If you're landing $100K contracts, you should buy a plane ticket, fly out, and visit them in person. Email is the leanest channel. Face-to-face is the richest channel.

PROVIDE THE SERVICE

"If the job's not done then it's not done,
but it will be done before I quit."

EMIL MOTYCKA

From 'Mow Boy' to $250K

Providing a service is the easiest way to make money. All you have to do is figure out what people need, see if you can do it, and place a bid.

If they hire you: provide the service, invoice them, and become more efficient over time. Services are simple.

Bid on Jobs

If you're providing a service, the main way you'll get jobs is by bidding on them. People who need work down will post the job, sometimes on sites like Elance.com and Freelancer.com, then service providers bid on the jobs.

Bidding on a job is the same as providing a quote or giving an estimate. It's an art. The only way you'll become good at it is by doing that type of work a lot. Keep track of how long it takes you to do certain jobs so you can bid more accurately in the future.

Eventually, you want to get away from having to bid on jobs because it's competitive and time-consuming. But this is where most service-providers start.

Get Hired

If you win a bid or have a customer come to you (because you did a good job of launching your business), congrats! Now that you've been hired, you have to set expectations, negotiate payment terms, and sign a contract.

1. **Set expectations.**
   As a service-provider, your client needs to know exactly what services you'll be providing, when you'll be providing them, and the level of quality that you'll deliver.

2. **Negotiate payment terms.**
   More often than not, you'll get paid once you complete the service. But if you're providing a service that has multiple levels until completion, require that you get paid a portion of the contract upfront. If you wait until you complete the entire contract, you risk not getting paid and not being able to pay your employees or contractors. The standard for a contract is 25%-50% upfront and the rest upon completion.

3. **Sign a contract.**
   Most simple services won't require a contract, but it's good to have one if your fee is over $1,000. It will let the client know exactly what they're paying for and it will protect you from legal issues. To make sure you have things in writing, always interact with your clients through email or record your phone calls. Refer to Chapter 9 if you want help writing a contract.

Once again, getting hired is usually as simple as, "I'll do this for you for this much." Then, "Ok, you're hired and I'll pay you when you're done."

Jacob Cass has his clients sign a contract no matter how small the graphic design job. For the smaller jobs (the smallest being $2200), they always pay 100% of the contract upfront. Since he's in such high demand as a graphic designer, he can negotiate these terms. This ensures that he gets the best clients and he always gets paid for the work.

Do it

Once you're hired, it's a matter of gitting-r-done. Do the job as quickly as possible. The client will be more satisfied with a faster service and it'll allow you to service more clients.

As a professional photographer, Lindsay Manseau is booked during the wedding season. It's important that she photographs the wedding and produces the photos as quickly as possible. If she procrastinates, she'll fall behind and all of her clients will be unhappy.

Bill and Invoice

As a business owner, it's your responsibility to get your clients to pay you. To get paid, send them an invoice. You have to tell them exactly how much to pay and you need to itemize everything you did in the invoice so they know exactly what they're paying for.

We'll get into the finer details of invoicing in the Chapter 8.

One area where Emil Motycka struggles is invoicing. His clients want to pay their bills weekly or monthly, but since he's still a full-time student, it's hard to get them out that often. Next year he is going to automate the invoicing system with FreshBooks.com which will be relatively easy because he mows once per week, every week

Set up Systems to Do it Better

As you provide the service over and over again, you'll find ways to make it more efficient. Nail down a process for providing the service that you can replicate for every client and train others to do for you.

Here are eight areas of your business that need to be systemized:

1. **Finding, qualifying, and contacting sales leads.**
   Find and contact them directly to try to get a sales meeting (push marketing). Or set up a website that collects leads with a conversion form as people visit (pull marketing).

2. **Conducting sales meetings.**
   You need a repeatable process that you go through with every potential client. Make a pamphlet or booklet with all of your services and prices to help them make a purchase decision.

3. **Keeping track of customer information.**
   Get a customer relationship management (CRM) system to help you keep track of customer information and communication. Salesforce.com is the leader in online CRM.

4. **Providing the service.**
   Document a step-by-step process for providing the service so you can easily train other people how to do it.

5. **Billing and invoicing.**
   Ideally, this should be automated so the customer will get a bill immediately after you provide the service.

6. **Following up with customer inquiries, requests, and feedback.**
   Customer support is important but it shouldn't eat up your day.

7. **Training and paying your employees.**
   If you can, hire multiple people at the same time so you can train them simultaneously. Then have them train the new hires. Like invoicing, payroll should be automated.

8. **Finding and qualifying new hires.**
   Once you discover a pool of qualified workers, harvest it.

You need to have a set process for each of those business activities. By documenting each of those processes, you'll be able to more easily run your business and train your employees.

In elementary school, Emil realized he could make $20 per hour mowing lawns. Not bad for a nine-year-old. Now at 22, Emil makes $60 per hour hiring other people to mow the lawns for him. He makes more money because he set systems in place to make his business run more efficiently. Since he can easily train new employees, he can focus on marketing, developing, and growing the business.

If you're looking for quick cash, provide a service. Look for the opportunities all around you. For example, after a windstorm, people will have fallen branches. Get a truck and stop by houses with damaged trees (starting in the rich neighborhoods). Then offer to remove and dispose of the branches for $50-$100. Think of your service as taking a weight off of their shoulders.

DELIVER THE PRODUCT

"A lot of the time the simple products are the ones that are really good. Complex products are great, but your first product needs to be simple or else you won't have the resources."

PHILIP HARTMAN

2008 Young Inventor of the Year

Most new business ideas are for products that are going to revolutionize the world. These insta-entrepreneurs are foolish. I know because I was one.

Products are much more complicated than services. They take time to make, they're harder to sell, and profit margins have to be razor slim to compete with corporations.

But if you create the right product and you market it effectively, it can be sold anytime, anywhere. That's recurring income, homie. This is the holy-grail of entrepreneurship.

Research and Development

The first step in creating the right product is to know exactly what the customer wants. You need to choose the perfect customer and know everything about them. This way you can develop the product to fit their exact needs.

Alex Fraiser started a blog about blogging because he wanted to teach people how to blog. He ran Blogussion.com for over a year and learned everything he could about bloggers. Several of his readers requested to purchase his design. Since he knew exactly what people wanted and saw that there was a demand for it, he developed a theme that he could sell. He made the right product and earned five-figures in the first month as a 16-year-old. The year leading up to the launch was all research and development as he learned what bloggers need in their designs.

Prototyping

Once you know exactly what people want and what they're willing to pay for, make a prototype. A prototype is the first version of your product. It won't have all the bells and whistles of the final product, but it will give you something to show to people. Plus, you'll find out if it's even possible to make.

Online, prototyping is referred to as the "beta" form of your software. When you label your software as "Beta" people know that you're still working on the final product.

Offline, your prototype might be a CAD (computer-aided design) drawing; a plastic rendering to show the size, shape, and design; or a fully functional prototype to show people how it works.

Philip Hartman, age 15, came up with the idea of wind-shield wipers that emit steam to defrost and clean windshields. As soon as he fleshed out the idea he went to Hobby Lobby to pick up parts for the prototype. By making a rough, but fully functional prototype he could demonstrate the product to potential investors and show that the technology works. Now he's looking for a large investment to ramp up manufacturing.

Manufacturing

If you can't efficiently mass produce the product yourself, you'll need to find a manufacturer. This is where a lot of entrepreneurs get stuck. They have a good idea and they've made the prototype, but finding a company to manufacture the product seems impossible.

It's not. Like spiders, manufacturing companies are looking for you more than you're looking for them. You are their business.

The first place to start on your quest for a manufacturer is your local SBDC (Small Business Development Center). They have contacts with local and overseas manufacturers. To find an SBDC near you, go to www.SBA.gov.

If you want to find and qualify manufacturers online, Alibaba.com and Thomasnet.com are the two largest databases for B2B manufacturing.

Coders and graphic designers are the internet-equivalent to manufacturers. You can find plenty of both on freelancing sites like Elance.com, 99designs.com, and oDesk.com.

Or you can make a website yourself with www.14clicks.com/click3.

When Adam Horwitz was developing his fourth online product, *Mobile Monopoly*, he started by doing all the development and design himself. It wasn't great. So he hired a graphic designer from Europe to redo everything. *Mobile Monopoly* went on to make $1.5 million in its three-day launch. Four months later he relocated that designer to Los Angeles where his company is based.

Packaging and Labeling

Now that you have a manufacturer, you need to figure out how you're going to package and label your product. You want to keep it simple.

The purpose of packaging is to hold and protect the product. Figure out what type of container your product fits best in. Maybe it's a bottle, a jar, a tin, or a box. With a simple Google search you will find thousands of companies that supply these containers.

Next find a labeling company that will design and print labels that you can peel and stick on those containers. The label needs to attract attention, describe the product, and communicate the benefits.

Custom packaging is about twice as expensive at minimum order quantities of about 500. If you think it's worth it, search for "custom packaging" and choose a vendor.

I haven't used it, but ActualPrint seems like a legitimate custom packaging vendor. To check out ActualPrint, go to www.ActualPrint.com.

Sabirul Islam, a best-selling 20-year-old author from the UK, sells a board game called Teen-Trepreneur. No one, including retailers, would buy a board game that comes in a generic, brown box. To professionally produce the board game he paid for custom design and packaging.

Getting into Retailers

Now you need to get your product in front of people who want to buy it. The best way to do that is to get it into a retail store, ideally a retail chain.

Start by making a list of all the local retailers where your customers shop. Then go shop-to-shop and ask to talk to the manager about getting your product in their store. You'll be surprised at how many of them will agree. They don't have a business unless they have products to sell.

Many of them will try to buy your product on consignment, meaning, you only get paid when it sells. That's a raw deal for you because you have to keep going back to the store. Try to get them to purchase it upfront. Keep in mind that they're going to keep 30-50% of the retail price. If they say no, start with consignment.

Once you make headway with local retailers, it's time to approach a retail chain. By getting into small retailers first you prove that your product sells. With this credibility the corporate retailers are going to be more likely to listen to you.

Get in contact with a buyer from the local retail chain and schedule a meeting with them. This is your opportunity to pitch your product and convince them why their store needs it. If they agree and the product does well, they'll ask if you can distribute it to their stores regionally. Then nationally.

My uncle, Mike Tart, owns a granola company called The Granola Guy. One day he was browsing the granola selection at REI and the store manager asked if she could help. He asked how they choose their suppliers. She told him that they're open to all sorts of local and non-local suppliers. Then he said, "I own a granola company. Would you mind if I gave you a free sample?" He went out to his car, grabbed an extra stash and gave it to her. She loved it and scheduled a meeting with him. Now it's being distributed in most of the REI's in Arizona.

Shipping Materials from Uline

In addition to retail, you need to sell your product online. Make an ecommerce website to sell your products. Then list them on other online retailers like Etsy, eBay, or Amazon. Find as many ways as you can to get your product in front of consumers.

When you start receiving orders, you need to pack and ship them. Uline is one of the world's largest suppliers of shipping materials and generic packaging. To find the best Uline materials to ship your products, go to www.Uline.com.

To ship our books we use Uline's Bubble Mailer #1 (product S-5632). It's the perfect size, it protects the books, it's self-adhesive, and it's pearly white.

Click-N-Ship with the US Postal Service

Have you been to the post office lately? If so, you probably noticed that it was full of old people. That's because all the cool kids know how to print postage and ship from home.

Click-N-Ship is the USPS service that lets you print your postage from home. The software is a little bulky but it works well for Express Mail, Priority Mail, and some international shipping.

To start printing postage online with Click-N-Ship, go to www.USPS.com.

> If I was running a business that needed to ship things especially fast, I would use Click-N-Ship. The downside to their service is that it only works for the fast and expensive shipping options.

Easier, Cheaper Shipping with Stamps.com

If you want to ship Media Mail or First-Class Mail (the two cheapest shipping options), then you need to use Stamps.com.

You can ship Media Mail (the cheapest shipping option) if you're mailing books, sound recordings, recorded video tapes, printed music, and recorded computer-readable media (such as CDs, DVDs, and diskettes). Media Mail takes 2-6 days if you're shipping in the Continental US.

If you're not shipping media, First-Class is the next cheapest option. You can only use First-Class if it's under 13 ounces. First-Class takes 1-3 days to arrive in the Continental US.

From a usability standpoint, Stamps.com is much easier and more efficient than Click-N-Ship. Just download their software, purchase postage, and start printing your labels. The only downside is that it costs $15.99 per month after the first month. Even then, it still beats going to the post office twice per week.

To sign up for a free trial, go to www.Stamps.com.

We use Stamps.com to ship our books. It used to take me a few hours to package the books, write out the addresses, and go to the post office. Now it takes about 15 minutes to print the labels and set them next to the mailbox.

If you're shipping from home, go to the post office and pick up a few white, plastic USPS bins that you can set next to your mailbox. The USPS gives them to you for free so you don't have to stuff your mailbox with your products and the mailman recognizes that you need to ship those items.

Shipping our books in white USPS bin.

ALWAYS OVER-DELIVER

"If you look at the statistics for our site, about 50% of our traffic comes from word of mouth… Girls telling girls — that's how we've expanded."

JULIETTE BRINDAK

$15 Million Valuation at 19 Years Old

Best marketing = Word of mouth

Word of mouth = Customer satisfaction

Customer satisfaction = Perceptions > Expectations

Best marketing = Perceptions > Expectations

In other words, always do a better job than what is expected of you and you will have an endless supply of customers.

Satisfy Customers 99% of the Time

The customer is always right, right? Generally that's the case. You want every customer to be very satisfied. If they tell you that they're unsatisfied, it gives you a chance to make things right. Most unsatisfied customers will never tell you but they will tell all of their friends.

Every once in awhile, you'll need to fire a customer. These are the people who are unreasonably knaggy, tell you how crummy your business is, and always complain that you did an unsatisfactory job. In the long run, these customers are costing you more money than they're worth.

If you have a bad customer, tell them, "Thank you for your business but we will no longer be serving you. As a customer, you're unsatisfied with our service so we recommend you change service-providers. We'd like to recommend (one of your competitors)."

One of the reasons Emil Motycka has been so successful is because he never leaves a job until it's 100% done and up to his standards. When Emil started analyzing the profit from his business, he realized that his landscaping service ($10,000+ contracts) was not as profitable as mowing lawns (at $20-40 per lawn). He no longer does landscaping jobs so he can focus on the most profitable portion of his company.

Provide Something Remarkable

Again, word of mouth is the best form of advertising. Here are three things you can do to encourage positive word of mouth.

1. **Sell your story as a young entrepreneur.**
   People like to be part of something extraordinary. More importantly, people like to tell others how they know extraordinary people. Ever heard one of your friends talk about how they played against a now professional athlete while in high school? As a young entrepreneur, you're remarkable. Make sure your customers know about your entrepreneurial journey. How you struggled in the beginning. When you had your turning point. Where you are today. That's the story that customers are going to share with their friends to make themselves seem cool.

2. **Provide referral incentives.**
   Tell all of your customers that if they refer business to you, you'll give them an incentive. Maybe it's 10% off the service or product. Maybe you can give them a gift card. They already want to talk about your business. Now they have incentive to do so. If you don't want them to feel uncomfortable about referring your business to others, tell them you'll give the same incentive to the customer they refer. This way everyone wins. The larger the incentive, the more people they'll refer.

3. **Make yourself sharable.**
   When you complete a project or finish a job, give your customers extra business cards that they can hand out to their friends. Print the referral incentive on these business cards and write the customer's name on the back so you know who referred them. On your site, make sure you have the Facebook "Like" button and the Twitter "Tweet" button. Do whatever you can to make it easy for customers to share your business or website.

Be unique. Do things other businesses don't. People talk about interesting things because it makes them seem interesting. Normal isn't interesting. Be cool.

When Johnny Cupcakes, a $3 million t-shirt brand, was just starting out, he fulfilled the t-shirt orders himself. He put Pokémon cards, batteries, potted plants, and whatever he found lying around the house in with the orders. He knew people (like I am right now) would talk about it. It didn't matter what the extra items were, the weirder, the more people talked about it.

According to NOP World, 93% of customers identified word of mouth as the best, most reliable source of information they use to make purchasing decisions. According to Keller Fay, the average person has 90 different brand conversations per week. Make sure your brand is at least a few of those conversations.

8

FIND YOUR FORTUNE

HOW TO COLLECT AND MANAGE YOUR MONEY

"I treat business a bit like a computer game. I count money as points. I'm doing really well: making lots of money and lots of points"

MICHAEL DUNLOP
Founder of Retire@21 and IncomeDiary

H aving a business is like having a pot of gold; except it's guarded by a stingy Leprechaun. You do and give, but he's reluctant to part with his fortune. Like gold-hoarding Leprechauns, customers don't like paying for things. Unlike Leprechauns, customers can reason.

Sometimes, one of the hardest parts of running a business is getting people to pay you. You won't have a problem with most customers but some will be stingy little Leprechauns. It's as though they know it's not worth your time and legal fees to go after them.

And when you do get paid, what do you do next? Do you pay yourself or do you put it back into the business?

Today, I'll tell you the most efficient ways to collect money, how to manage it, and how to fund the growth of your business.

CASH FLOW IS KING

"I want to have several different online revenue streams that for the most part automate them-selves. I'll have a certain level of income guaranteed coming in every day and I could sleep and it would still come in."

ALEX MAROKO
From $0 to $100K in Five Months

Imagine if you worked for a week but didn't get paid until three months later. Ridiculous, right?

In some cases, that's how the business world works.

When we sell a book on Amazon, it's six months before we get paid. Amazon waits 90 days to pay publishers. Then our publisher pays us quarterly. Since it takes so long for us to get paid, we have to keep a retainer in the business account so we can buy more books before we get paid for the ones we already sold.

A lack of cash flow is one of the main reasons businesses fail.

There's not much you can do about it. Just take this into consideration and try to develop a business model that gets paid immediately for what you sell.

COLLECT THE BENJAMINS

"I was young and stupid. The money was coming in so strongly, but it went out just as fast."

ANDREW FASHION
Made and Spent $2.5 Million by 21

I don't like asking for money.

When I have to collect, I get clammy and uncomfortable. My voice sputters like a 14-year-old asking a girl to homecoming. It would be so much easier to do work for free, but that's not how business works.

These tips will make it easier and less awkward to collect your earnings.

Charge Upfront

Unlike employees, sometimes entrepreneurs get paid before they do anything. That's the way it should be, but it doesn't always work out like that.

As I mentioned in Chapter 7, get paid before you do the work. It'll solve some of your cash flow woes and it will motivate you to get the work done. Typically, freelancers get paid 25-50% of the contract upfront with the rest to be paid upon completion.

If you sell a product, it's less complicated. The customer pays for and gets the product simultaneously.

> When Emil Motycka was doing $5K-10K landscaping jobs, he trusted his customers so he didn't charge upfront. He still has several clients who owe him thousands of dollars for work he did years ago.

Accept Cash in Person

Before you start accepting cash in person, go to Walmart and get a $5 receipt book. When a customer buys something from you, ask if they want a receipt.

With the receipt book you can quickly write up a receipt, tear off the top carbon-copy, and you both have receipts for your records.

> I have a box in my car with 30 books, packing materials, a container to keep the money, and a receipt book. This way, I can sell books wherever I go.

Accept Credit Cards in Person

Traditionally, to accept credit cards you needed a merchant account from your bank. The annual fee alone is a couple hundred bucks.

As I mentioned in Chapter 7, the best way to accept credit cards in person is with the Square (as long as you have a Smartphone). The Square plugs into your phone and processes credit cards through an app. Then your customer signs the phone with their finger. Within seconds, they get an email receipt. To get a free Square, go to SquareUp.com.

> When we do speaking engagements, we sell our book afterwards. Most people don't have cash. So we give them a book, take their email address, and send them a PayPal invoice when we got home. As you can imagine, a few of those people never ended up paying. When I get a Smartphone, I'm getting a Square.

Flexible Payment Terms

Offering flexible payment terms is one way you can make customers happy. Generally when a customer gets an invoice, you should give them 15 or 30 days to pay. To get them to pay sooner, offer a small discount if they pay in so many days.

For instance, if you write "2/10 net 30" on a $500 invoice, that customer can take a 2% discount ($10) if they pay within ten days. If they don't take the discount, the bill is due in 30 days.

> For his lawn customers, Emil Motycka had "net 30" payment terms. However, this year he's bumping it to net 15 because he needs the cash to grow. Only in rare occasions would he offer the discount.

Make an Invoice with Word

The old-fashioned way to make an invoice is to download a template for Microsoft Word. Then simply fill out the invoice and adjust it to fit your business.

It takes 30 minutes to download the template, customize the invoice, print it out, and mail it in. You also need to include a self-addressed stamped envelope (SASE).

To find free Microsoft Word invoice templates, go to Office.Microsoft.com.

> Last summer I was a contractor for the local Workforce Center. When the contract was complete, I made an invoice in Microsoft Word, added my logo, and mailed it in. I didn't get paid until a month later.

Easier Invoicing with PayPal

Now that we have the internet, requesting money and sending invoices is simple. PayPal lets you easily create and save invoice templates that you email to your customers and clients. This allows them to pay with a credit card so they can rack up those rewards.

To send a business invoice with PayPal, set up a free Business PayPal account and click "Request Money" → "Create Invoice." To get started with PayPal, go to www.PayPal.com.

Pre-Blogussion, Alex Fraiser was doing freelance blog design. To invoice his clients, he used PayPal. But since he was under 18 (only 15 at the time), PayPal shut him down. So he had his dad create a PayPal account and his clients paid his dad. Then his dad paid him.

Professional Invoicing with FreshBooks

The most professional invoicing service I have ever found is FreshBooks.com. It's the perfect tool for freelancers and invoicing is a small part of its functionality.

With FreshBooks, you can choose to invoice your clients through email or mail. If they want to get it in the mail, FreshBooks will print out the invoice and mail it to your client. Then your client gets a professional invoice with a perforated bill and a self-addressed envelope to easily mail the check back to you.

FreshBooks also integrates with PayPal for email invoicing. To get started with a free FreshBooks account, go to www.FreshBooks.com.

Emil Motycka is setting up his FreshBooks account for this mowing season. It'll let him automatically invoice all of his clients on a weekly basis as soon as the lawn is mowed. Plus, his staff can login, upload their hours, and Emil can easily pay them with a few clicks.

Shopping Cart for eCommerce

Accepting credit cards on your site is more complicated than you would think. If you process the orders yourself, then you're liable for securing your customers' credit card information.

Most entrepreneurs opt to integrate shopping carts with their website. This isn't easy either.

If you're not a coder or don't have a budget to hire one, your best option for setting up an online store is Shopify. They let you easily create good-looking, customizable storefronts and they streamline the checkout process so you don't lose customers. Plus, they guarantee that your store is super secure.

To get your Shopify free trial, go to www.Shopify.com.

However, if your site is built on WordPress, you should use the WP e-Commerce plugin for your shopping cart.

To check out WPEC, www.GetShopped.org.

Matthew Inman, the 27-year-old founder of *The Oatmeal*, uses Shopify to host and process his orders. He gets over five million people per month to his site and makes a full-time income from selling posters, t-shirts, coffee mugs, and his best-selling book.

Make sure all the money that your business collects goes into your business bank account. If you decide to pay yourself, do a money transfer from the business into your personal account. Do this and taxes will be much less of a hassle because you can easily track your revenue.

MANAGE THE BENJAMINS

"There have been so many times when I almost failed. When we first started, we were taking in money but we didn't know how to manage it. Nothing was organized. But something always told me to keep going and find a way to make it work."

BEN WEISSENSTEIN
Founder of Grand Slam Garage Sales

Every year, my family and I eat black-eyed peas on New Year's Eve. Supposedly, you earn $100 over the next year for every black-eyed pea you eat.

It's not completely irrational. As you get older you're willing to cram down more those disgusting peas. But I don't have any stats to prove it.

Besides testing family traditions, there are more reasons to keep track of your earnings.

Why Keep Track?

Keeping track of money is a burden. It's hard to be diligent enough to list every expense, keep every receipt, and track every dollar. But you need to do it for three reasons.

1. **To make tax season easier.**
   If you don't itemize your expenses and monitor every penny, you're going to pay a lot more taxes than you need to. Keep 30% of your profit in the business savings account for taxes.

2. **To benchmark year to year.**
   Don't you want to know exactly how much your business makes? By knowing your stats, you can set more accurate goals and make better decisions for your business.

3. **Because Inc. needs to know.**
   If you want to be in Inc. Magazine's 30 under 30, you need to be able to prove every dollar that you say you've earned.

Josh Shipp made Inc.'s *30 Under 30* list in 2009 at the age of 28. In order to be considered, Inc. required that their people go through all of his financials. They found that he made $580,000 in 2008 and was projected to make $1.8 million in 2009.

Simple Spreadsheet

When you're first starting out, a simple Excel spreadsheet will do. Make an inventory tab, an expense tab, and a revenue tab. Then link them all together to make a profit tab.

Every week, update that spreadsheet with your inventory counts, expenses, and revenues. If you have hard-copy receipts, organize them into a folder.

Ben Weissenstein told us, "We knew we had to keep records to an extent, so we started by opening a Word document and writing, 'We took in x amount of dollars, we had x amount of expenses.' Eventually that turned into a nice Excel spreadsheet, which turned into software that we had developed so we could put in [financial] information."

Easy Money Tracking with FreshBooks

If you want to be diligent and professional about tracking your money from the outset, start by using FreshBooks. They make it easy to track your money. Plus, you can reports so you can see all sorts of financial statistics for your company.

To get started with FreshBooks for free, go to www.FreshBooks.com.

The software that Ben Weissenstein paid to have developed for his business is comparable to what FreshBooks gives you for free. Once you have more than three regular clients, they start charging for it. But at that point, you can afford it.

> Most entrepreneurs don't give themselves a proper salary (about $40K) until their business makes $250K in profit. Up to that point, pull out only as much as you need to survive.

FUND YOUR FORTUNE

"This time, instead of blowing money on toys and cars, I am going to invest it back into the company or another company."

ANDREW FASHION
Made and Lost $2.5 Million by 21

The real value to being an entrepreneur is that you can invest money back into your business. It's like buying stock in yourself. This is how entrepreneurs amass their fortunes.

You may have noticed that this is the first time I've talked about funding your startup. I believe every business should be self-funded from the outset as much as you can.

Once you've proven the business, you can attract investors. Even better, once you've become profitable, you can reinvest that money to grow the business.

How Much do You Need?

Maybe you need equipment to run your business more efficiently. Maybe you need a better website to get more sales. Maybe you want a hired hand so you can focus on growing the business.

Before you invest in your startup, know how much you need and the reasons why you need it.

When Michael Dunlop launched IncomeDiary, he started with a $70 theme from WooThemes.com. In the first month, he made $5K and now he has a six-figure income from that site. Since he started, Michael has invested over $30K in redesigning IncomeDiary.com to what it is today.

Forecast Profitability of Investment

To determine if an investment is worth it, you need to predict the future value of the investment.

For instance, if you think your $50K business can run twice as efficiently and you can land the additional sales with a $10K investment, that's a good decision.

If you're blog is only making a couple hundred dollars a month and you want to hire a professional designer for $5K, you better be able to justify why a $5K design will improve your business 10-20 fold.

Michael Dunlop was willing to spend a cars-worth of money to redesign IncomeDiary because he knew he would recoup his investment. A slick, customized design is one thing that separates the hobbyists from the professionals. If he wanted to develop a community of people who consider him to be a professional, he needed to upgrade his $70 theme to something sleeker.

Self-Funding

Let's say you've determined that you should invest in your business. Where does that money come from?

If you're doing things correctly, it should come from the business. Maybe you eat Ramen noodles and ketchup for a month. If that's what it takes, then do it.

Another option is maxing out a few credit cards. I know, I know. That goes against everything your mother taught you. Just hear me out. If you only need a couple grand and don't have cash, you have three options:

1. **Friends and family.**
   Asking for money from friends and family is sketchy and you risk losing relationships.

2. **Bank loan.**
   Bank loans require a business plan and tons of paperwork. Then they take 30 days to process. Best case scenario, you get the loan and they charge average interest rates.

3. **Credit cards.**
   It takes 30 seconds to get approved for a credit card (assuming you have a good credit score). Plus, you can probably get a lower initial interest rate than the bank would offer. If you know for a fact that you can pay off those credit cards in a month or two, it's a no-brainer.

A few months back, a friend of mine applied for a dozen credit cards in one day. If you get them all at the same time, it doesn't affect your credit score as much. Each card had a $20-$40,000 limit and they all started with low interest rates. In one day, he effectively received a quarter-million dollars in startup capital without giving up a penny of equity and with lower interest rates than the bank.

Again, the only reason he could do this was because he had been running the business for over a year and he knew he could recoup the money with the extra capital. Plus, they were willing to give him $20,000-$40,000 limits because he had a solid credit score from always paying off his credit cards.

Disclaimer: Don't do this without doing more legal research. The point here is to think of creative ways to fund your company.

Finding an Investor

Too many entrepreneurs seek funding from outside sources before they need it and they give up a butt-load of equity in their business. Only on rare occasions (e.g. Facebook, Twitter, Groupon, etc.) should you need an investor.

If you believe you're the next Facebook, Twitter, or Groupon, you will find two types of investors:

1. **Angel Investors**
   Angels typically invest in the $50K-500K range. These are independently-wealthy people who don't invest in companies for a living, but they're looking for good ways to use their money. If they like you and think that it's a solid investment, they'll give you the cash. But you have to give up a hearty portion of your business to get it, especially if you don't have any skin in the game.

2. **Venture Capitalists (VCs)**
   If you need more than a half-million dollars, start looking for VCs. Many of them have private equity firms. Try contacting them yourself, but don't be surprised if you have to jump through hoops just to set up a meeting.

Most of the time investors will give you an option to buy them out after three-five years. They're not looking for long-term investments. They want to give you money upfront with the expectation that they'll soon get it back (plus a hefty return). Make sure you have the buy-back option guaranteed in the contract in case your business takes off and they want to stick around.

After Andrew Fashion lost his $2.5 million, he needed $145,000 for his next venture. He didn't have any cash. In his heyday, some of his friends stole cash from him, so he couldn't go there. Banks wouldn't listen to a 21-year-old kid who threw away $2.5 million. And he wasn't about to get approved for a credit card with his credit score.

His only option was to find an investor. So he used his blog to showcase his previous success and let everyone know that he was looking for an investor. Within a month, a local angel investor contacted him, they set up a meeting, and he landed his $145,000. With that, he launched beModel.com.

Emil Motycka's mentor told him that one of the biggest business mistakes he ever made was prematurely giving up equity in his company. You get a lot of added respect and much needed capital when you land an investor, but you lose ownership and control of your company. Don't give up ownership in your business unless you've exhausted every other option.

9

LEGAL MUMBO JUMBO

EVERYTHING FROM LICENSES TO LLCS

"I'm willing to do everything that it takes to succeed – as long as it's moral and legal."

BEN WEISSENSTEIN
Founder of Grand Slam Garage Sales

D *isclaimer: I'm not a lawyer (nor do I want to be). If you're in sticky legal terrain, I recommend that you grab professional advice.*

But that doesn't mean I'm completely clueless when it comes to the laws of the land. In fact, it's essential that every business owner has a grasp of certain legal basics – otherwise, someone could steal your idea or skip out on your contract.

> In most cases, don't worry about the legalities of your business until you become profitable. It'll just trip you up when you should be moving forward. Until then, it's a sole proprietorship.

By the end of this chapter, you'll know everything you need to know about:

- Licenses
- Permits
- Patents
- Trade names
- Limited Liability Companies (LLCs)
- Employer Identification Numbers (EINs)
- Business bank accounts
- Insurance
- Contracts
- Taxes
- Certified Public Accountants (CPAs)
- Lawyers
- and chocolate frogs.

Ok, maybe not chocolate frogs.

I've even enlisted the help of an expert to make this part as solid as it can be. When you find a nugget of particularly helpful advice, thank Carol Topp (a CPA and the owner of MicroBusinessForTeens.com).

Editor's note: Laws are different all over the world. The legal information below is only useful in the United States. If you're doing business in another country, seek information about the laws of that country.

BUSINESS LICENSES & PERMITS

*"It's easier to ask forgiveness than
it is to get permission."*

GRACE HOPPER
Developed the First Computer Programming Compiler

Not all licenses and permits are created equal.

Your driver's license doesn't give you a license to drive a motorcycle.

Most businesses don't require any license whatsoever, but it's better to be safe than sorry.

Federal Regulations

In the US, the national government requires that you have a license in the areas of, "agriculture, alcohol, aviation, firearms and explosives, fish & wildlife, maritime transportation, mining & drilling, nuclear energy and radio and TV production."

If this sounds like your business, find out more at www.Business.gov.

State Requirements

If you want to be a lawyer, doctor, architect, electrician, or beautician, you'll need a license from your state. This is your state's way of making sure that the professionals you enlist to cut your hair or design your house actually knows what they're doing.

If you want to provide any sort of repair service, you might need to get a contractor's license (depending on your state). Like most licenses, you have to take a few classes and pass a test.

To find out if you need a state license, go to www.Business.gov.

Local Licenses

Your city or county will require licenses or permits for some local businesses. Common examples include vendor's licenses (a.k.a. seller's permit, sales tax license, sales and use tax license), health permits, and zoning permits. So, if you're selling a product, cooking something, or working out of your home, there's a good chance that your local government is regulating it.

To make sure that you're on the right side of your state and local law, go to www.Business.gov.

Getting Your Vendor's License

If you're selling a product in person to people in your state, you'll need a vendor's license. Get this license from your local government. To find out where you can get a vendor's license, search "City of (your town) business tax license."

Follow the online instructions and pay for it (about $25 depending on your city). If you have any issues, they should have contact info on that page.

> Since we're selling our book at events in town, we need to collect sales tax. In order to collect sales tax, we need a vendor's license from the City of Fort Collins.

A vendor's license is relatively simple to acquire and it's the one thing you'll definitely need if you're selling a product.

PATENTED PROTECTION

"I never perfected an invention that I did not think about in terms of the service it might give others. I find out what the world needs, then I proceed to invent."

THOMAS EDISON
Inventor and Founder of General Electric

A patent is like a fortress around your castle to prevent the world's biggest corporations from coming inside and stealing your damsel.

What is a Provisional Patent?

Technically, there's no such thing as a *provisional patent*. You can file a *provisional application for patent* which includes a description and drawings of your invention. It proves that you had the idea when you actually had the idea.

Once you file your provisional application, you have 12 months to finalize the invention and complete the patent process. As of March 14, 2011 it costs $330 to file a provisional application. Generally, patents will protect your invention for 20 years.

Types of Patents

All patents fall under one of three categories:

1. **Utility Patent (Most common)**
   To protect a new invention or product.

2. **Design Patent**
   To protect a new or original design for something you manufacture that's different than the design of similar products.

3. **Plant Patent**
   To protect a new variety of plant you develop or invent. Like flowers and herbs.

Filing a Patent

If you want to patent your product, start with filing a provisional application. You can do this online at the United States Patent and Trademark Office.

To file a provisional application for patent, go to www.USPTO.gov.

Once you have your provisional application and you've proven the concept, spend the $20,000 or so to hire a patent attorney to make everything official.

Philip Hartman filed his provisional application for SteamTech and he's pulling together a list of investors and customers before he files for the actual patent.

> Before you invest in a full patent, sell a few copies of the invention to make sure that it's something people actually want.

BE A LEGITIMATE COMPANY

"Talking to friends and people on the internet who have already done it – that's the best resource that you can get."

MARSHALL HAAS
20-Year-Old Architect Outsourcer

Ready to play with the big kids?

Becoming a legitimate company gives you credibility and it protects you from getting sued if a customer wants to pick a fight.

Is it a Hobby?

The line between a hobby and a for-profit endeavor is blurry. It depends on your motive.

If you're doing it to make a profit, then the IRS considers it a business. If you're doing it for the love and enjoyment of the activity (and happen to make money), then it's a hobby. The IRS looks to see if you've spent money on advertising or have received professional help. If so, to them you're operating a business.

To get further clarification, go to www.IRS.gov.

Lindsay Manseau is a professional photographer. When she's shooting weddings and portraits, Lindsay is operating as a business. But if she takes a few scenic photos for fun and someone happens to buy one, then it's a hobby.

Doing Business As...Trade Name

Bruce Wayne's trade name is Batman. Your trade name is the name of your company.

If you don't want someone stealing your company name, then you should reserve it through your Secretary of State. Once that's done, nobody else in your state will be able to do business under that name.

How to Reserve Your Trade Name

Before you reserve your trade name, make sure you've finalized the name of your company. By finalized, you should put "LLC" at the end of it (e.g. 14 Clicks, LLC) because you will be a Limited Liability Company.

Once you feel confident with it, go ahead with the name reservation process:

1. **See if your trade name is available.**
   Go to your state's Secretary of State website and find where you can "reserve a name." Perform a name availability search with exactly how it will appear on your legal documents (e.g. 14 Clicks, LLC). If your name is available, move forward with reserving it.

2. **Fill out the "Statement of Reservation of Name."**
   Find and fill out the "Statement of Reservation of Name." Some states let you do this online while others require you to print it out and send it in. There's a small fee, about $10-$50 to reserve your name. Pay it and print out the confirmation page for your records.

Limited Liability Company

An LLC is like a legal blanket for business. If you make a mistake as an LLC and someone decides to sue you, they can only sue your company. They can't touch your college savings account or any other personal assets.

Also, some clients prefer not to do business with you unless you're an official company.

How to Register Your LLC

After you register your LLC, your business will be an official bona fide company. Some states let you do this online, and others make you fill it out and mail it in.

When filing your LLC, make sure that you use the exact same name as you registered. That includes punctuation, capitalization, and spelling.

1. **File "Articles of Organization (LLC)."**
   Register your LLC back at your state's Secretary of State website. There you'll find a link that reads, "File a new limited liability company" or some variation. Click it and you'll be taken to where you can fill out the "Articles of Organization (LLC)" form. Fill out the entire document and submit it.

2. **Pay and print.**
   Depending on your state, it'll be free or up to $1,000. Typically it's in the $25-100 range. If it costs you $1,000, consider moving to a state that's friendlier to entrepreneurs. Pay the man and print out the confirmation page for your records.

When I reserved my name and LLC in Colorado, it cost $75 and took about an hour. Some well-known companies charge $1,000-2,000 to do this for you. Be wary and look out for these businesses.

Employer ID Number or Employer Tax ID

Your EIN number is like a social security number for your business. You'll use it to file taxes and work as an independent contractor. It's free to set up and it's good to have so you don't have to use your social security number on your business forms.

To get a free EIN (and use it for all of your businesses), go to www.IRS.gov.

When I got my EIN, I saved that number in my phone as EINstein. You should too. You'll need to use it a few times a year, which isn't often enough to memorize it. Plus, your friends will be impressed that you have Einstein's number.

Just because your official business name ends in an LLC, this doesn't mean you have to put "LLC" at the end of your name every time you use it. Only use "LLC" on checks and other official documents. Put it in the footer of your marketing materials, but don't put it in your logo. It will build credibility, but from a branding perspective, it's ugly and annoying. "LLC" isn't in my logo but it is in the footer of 14clicks.com.

BANK AS A BUSINESS

"I'm living at home still. I don't have to pay for rent or anything, so I can just put it in the bank. Stay at home as long as you can, even if you're making a lot of money. Don't stay until you're 30, though. And if you're 60: you gotta be out."

ADAM HORWITZ
Made $1.5 Million in Three Days at 18

Banks give more than just free suckers. Read carefully so you'll be prepared to cash-in on free upgrades.

As long as you're over 18, you can set up a free business savings and checking account. If you're under 18, you'll need to have your parents or guardians co-sign on the account and sign the checks.

Why You Need a Business Bank Account

Set up a bank account for your business to keep your business expenses separate from your personal expenses. This way, you'll be able to write off your business expenses so you don't have to pay taxes on those amounts.

Make sure that your bank or credit union gives you a business credit/debit card. Then use that card for all of your business expenses to easily keep track.

When Ben Weissenstein started Grand Slam Garage Sales, he was under 18. So his mom had to cash all the checks. But he could still make business purchases with his business credit and debit cards.

It's important to keep money in your savings account for tax reasons (about 30% of your profit). As an employee, you're company holds back some taxes from your paycheck. But as an employer, you have to be ready to pay the taxman come April.

Choose a Bank

If you already have a personal bank account, set up your business account with the same bank. By doing this, you'll be able to easily (usually online) pay yourself and transfer money between accounts.

If you don't have any bank accounts, here are a few of the nation's largest and most reputable banks:

- Bank of America
- J.P. Morgan Chase & Company
- Citigroup
- Wells Fargo & Company
- HSBC North America Inc.
- Or you can bank with your local credit union.

We Bank with Wells Fargo

Our official recommendation is Wells Fargo & Company for six reasons:

1. Every time I visit, I'm greeted by a friendly staff (no matter what branch).

2. I've made several mistakes that led to fees, and they went back and "corrected" them.

3. The only fee I have is $12.50/year to be a part of their rewards program.

4. Online banking is a breeze.

5. They are nationwide so you can always find a Wells Fargo no matter where your business takes you.

6. Free suckers, every time. And even a cookie, once. It was chocolate-chocolate chip and they baked it in the store.

To find a local Wells Fargo branch, go to www.WellsFargo.com.

How to Set Up Your Business Bank Account

Setting up your business bank account might be intimidating at first. To make it less intimidating and to get as many free upgrades as possible, go through this process.

1. **Find and go to your local Wells Fargo branch.**
    If you're under 18, you'll need to bring a parent or legal guardian. Bring two forms of ID, your official documents (LLC and EIN), and at least $100 for the initial deposit.

2. **Talk to the business banker.**
    When you get there, ask to talk to the business banking representative. Tell them about your business and they'll set you up with the best banking option for your business. Ask if there are any fees and what you can do to waive them. Then ask for a set of free starter checks so you can use them right away.

3. **Thank them and get their contact info.**
    Having a solid relationship with a banker will be valuable to your business down the road. They can pull a lot of strings for

you. So make sure you thank them and get their business card.

Grab a free sucker on the way out.

> When Emil Motycka started mowing lawns as a nine-year-old, he didn't have a trade name, an LLC, or a bank account. It was a hobby. But as his lawn care business grew, Emil reserved a trade name (Motycka Enterprises), made it into an LLC (Motycka Enterprises, LLC), and set up a business bank account. By the time Emil was a senior in high school, Motycka Enterprises, LLC made $135,000 in one summer. Now he has multiple businesses and separate bank accounts for each one.

> When you open your business account, make a deposit from your personal savings that's large enough to cover your startup costs. Treat this initial deposit as a loan from yourself to your business with the intention for your business to pay back that loan as soon as it gets revenue.

BE SURE WITH INSURANCE

"Fun is like life insurance; the older you get, the more it costs."

KIN HUBBARD
19th Century American Cartoonist

Operating a business without insurance is like crossing America in a covered wagon without a spare wheel.

You can do it, but it's risky.

General Liability Insurance

Registering as an LLC covers your liability as a company. But some customers, especially commercial clients, will require that you have general liability insurance as well.

Essentially, you pay the insurance company a small, monthly fee so that they'll cover the cost of damages if someone or something is ever damaged because of your product or service.

Emil Motycka pays about $100 per month for general liability insurance against all of his equipment and he has separate automobile insurance for his five trucks.

Home-Based Business Insurance

A standard homeowner's insurance policy typically covers some damages incurred by having a home-based business. But if you want your business to be completely covered, home-based business insurance is a more robust alternative.

We don't have general liability insurance or home-based business insurance for 14 Clicks because there's not much risk that the website is going to hurt anyone (no sharp edges).

There's a good chance that you won't need any type of insurance for your business, especially if it doesn't involve expensive or dangerous equipment. Before you make a decision, it's best to consult a legal professional.

CONTRACT ME

"A verbal contract isn't worth the paper it's printed on."

SAM GOLDWYN

20th Century American Film Producer

Get everything in writing.

You've heard it a thousand times. But you won't take that advice seriously until a customer or contractor that weasels out of a $1,000+ deal that you made over the phone.

Not Binding as a Minor

Never make a contract with someone who is under 18 years old. They're not legally bound by contracts. Have their parents or a business mentor sign the contract instead.

At 15 years old, Philip Hartman is looking for investors. It's tough because he can't legally make a deal with anyone. So his parents have to be involved, which makes it hard for investors to take him seriously.

Writing a Contract

Here are seven things your contract should have:

1. A detailed **description the type of work** to be done.

2. A specific **price and payment** arrangement.

3. A clearly worded plan that describes individual **tasks and deliverables**.

4. A schedule with **dates and deadlines**.

5. An agreement as to **who owns the rights** to what you are creating (i.e. the website files).

6. **Terms to get out** of the contract.

7. **Dated signatures** from all parties.

Andrew Fashion hired a developer and designer to build beModel.com. Since he trusted them to do a good job, he didn't flesh out a detailed contract. Their work wasn't up to par. Now he's left redoing the site himself and he's out $50,000.

Free Contract Templates

If you don't want to waste time trying to figure out all the nuisances with writing a complete contract, there are a bunch of places online that have free template contracts.

Search for "(your service) free contract templates" and you'll find plenty. Download and adjust them to fit your business.

Cheap, Professional Contracts with DocStoc

You can get away with the free contracts in the beginning but eventually you'll need to make customized contracts for your business. One of the easiest ways to do that is find a contract that fits your business model as closely as possible, then rework it a little.

You are more likely to find the perfect contract with a paid service. Once you can afford it, I suggest upgrading to more professional contracts. The world's largest database of professional contracts is DocStoc.com. Access to unlimited downloads ranges from $9.95 to $19.95 per month.

To find cheap contract templates, go to www.DocStoc.com.

> Emil Motycka grows his company by acquiring smaller companies. These contracts have to consider lost customers during the transition to his company. All the contracts are specific to the businesses involved so he writes them himself.

> Contracts aren't one-size-fits-all. If you want to ensure that your contract covers all of the bases and is completely legally binding, seek legal counsel.

TAXES TO UNCLE SAM

"In this world nothing can be said to be certain, except death and taxes."

BENJAMIN FRANKLIN
Co-Founder of The United States of America

Taxes stink. Depending on how much you make, you can owe up to 1/3 of it back to the government.

But if you think of it as paying for a service that your business needs (e.g. roads to drive on, a pre-educated work force, etc.), it's not as bad.

Federal Income Tax

If you make $5,700 or more in a calendar year, you will need to pay federal income tax. This income can come from being an employee or from owning a business. $5,700 is the typical amount of a deduction for a single person. It's adjusted by a few hundred dollars every year.

Americans report their income and tax due on a Form 1040. Business owners report their profit on a Form 1040 Schedule C Profit or Loss from Business.

If your LLC performed as a partnership with two or more people, you'll need to file a Form 1065. And each of you needs to fill out a Form K-1 and a Schedule E.

Self-Employment Tax – The Hidden Tax

If you're self-employed or own a business and earn more than $400 a year in profit, then you need to know this easy-to-miss tax.

The SE tax is 15.3% of your profit. So, if your business makes $1000, you'll have to pay $153 in Self-Employment taxes – even though your earnings are below the $5700 threshold for paying federal income tax.

This tax goes towards paying Social Security and Medicare.

In addition to the Form 1040 and the Profit or Loss from Business, you need to file the Schedule SE for self-employment.

Keeping Good Records

To get started, use Microsoft Excel to keep track of your expenses, revenues, and profits. Every time you purchase something for your business, make sure you use your business credit/debit card. This is important to track how well your business is doing and so you'll know exactly how much taxes you'll have to pay.

You can find more details on keeping track of your finances in Chapter 8.

Ben Weissenstein paid a company to have software developed for his garage sale service because his business quickly became more complicated than Excel and QuickBooks.com.

Filing Taxes

Every year, by April 15th, you have to pay taxes on the profit you earned January 1st – December 31st of the previous year.

No matter what, everyone has to fill out a Form 1040. As a business owner, you have to file the Schedule SE as well. In addition to the Form 1040 and Schedule SE, you'll have to file one of these three forms:

1. If you had business **expenses less than $5,000** during the year, had **no inventory**, and operated as a **sole proprietor**, then you can use the Schedule C-EZ to file your taxes. This is the "EZ"est form to fill out.

2. If you have are the **sole owner** of your company/LLC, you'll have to file the Form 1040 Schedule C Profit or Loss.

3. If your company performed as a **partnership** with two or more members, you'll need to file a Form 1065. Then each member will have to fill out a Form K-1 and a Schedule E. Partnerships are complicated, with taxes and with running the business.

Once you download and fill out the forms, attach them to your Form 1040 and mail them back to the IRS. To find out where you send your forms, go to www.IRS.gov.

Easier Taxes with TurboTax

If you want to skip the hassle of choosing the right forms, guessing at what numbers to put in, and hoping to send them to the right place, use TurboTax.

Besides knowing that you did your taxes right, TurboTax will help you itemize your expenses to make sure you get as many tax deductions as possible. There is a fee to use their service, but you should easily recoup that fee with the money you save from the deductions (not to mention the time you save).

TurboTax has two options for entrepreneurs, "Home & Business" and "Business." To check them out, go to www.TurboTax.com.

> Carol Topp says, "as a rough rule of thumb, save 25-30% of your profit to pay your federal income tax and your self-employment tax."

SEEK OUT OTHER RESOURCES

"Young entrepreneurs need to nail down the art of networking. Some of my best opportunities have come out of those cold-call approaches."

LAUREN AMARANTE
Co-Founder of World Entrepreneurship Day

Like the business world, the legal world is constantly changing. By now you have a basic understanding of how to cover your legal grounds, but these resources will help even more.

Call Your Local Government

Go to your local government's website (e.g. http://fcgov.com/business/) and look for contact information for a small business representative. If you can't find it, search for "City of (your town) business." They will be able to give you the best, most accurate information that you can get.

Call them, let them know what you're doing, and ask them to give you a list of everything you need to cover your legal basis. Then ask them if they can direct you to where you can acquire your licenses.

Certified Public Accountants

A CPA will help you make sure you're doing all of your bookkeeping and filing correctly. They charge anywhere from $50-$300 per hour, so it's not cheap. But getting audited because you did something wrong or filed your taxes incorrectly will cost you much more.

Take your first $100 of profit and visit a CPA. You might get an hour with them for free if you play your "helpless young entrepreneur" card right.

Both Syed Balkhi and Michael Dunlop have CPA's who do all of their financial stuff. Everything from tracking the money, to paying their employees, to filing taxes. This way they can focus on the things they're good at.

Small Business Lawyer

Eventually, you're going to need a lawyer. It's best to build a relationship with a lawyer as soon as you can.

Find a reputable small business lawyer in your community. Schedule an introductory meeting with them and make sure they know that it's an opportunity to help out a young entrepreneur. Typically, they'll give you the first half hour for free, especially if you're a young person.

More Advice from Carol Topp

Here is a collection of other resources that Carol has pulled together.

1. *Starting a Micro Business*: Will help you plan and launch a successful micro business.

2. *Running a Micro Business*: Will help you in the day-to-day of running your micro business.

3. **Micro Business for Teens Workbook**: To help teens implement what you've learned from S*tarting a Micro Business* and *Running a Micro Business.*

4. ***Teens and Taxes***: Learn about the taxes that affect teenagers in an easy to understand way.

Find them all at www.MicroBusinessForTeens.com.

Syed Balkhi's lawyer, finance guy, and insurance guy are all clients of his. A surefire way to get free, professional services is to help people who can help you.

> If you contact a CPA or a lawyer and they're not willing to sit down for an initial meeting for free, you don't want to give them business. Call someone else until you find one who will.

10

GROW

EARN A SPOT IN OUR NEXT BOOK

"Up to this last week, I had been doing it all myself – which was a bit crazy. I finally got a guy who helps me to edit and shoot."

JOE PENNA
YouTube's Mystery Guitar Man

When you were ten years old, $100 seemed like a lot. It could get you anything you wanted. Now that you're 5-10-15-20 years older, it takes more than $100 to feed your fancy.

The same concept applies to your business. Your once-a-month design jobs aren't going to cut it forever. If you're not growing, you're not an entrepreneur. You have a job. Start a business that can be scaled and run a business with the intent to grow.

By the end of the chapter you'll know what it means to become an entrepreneur, the five ways to grow your business, and how to manage that growth once it starts to take off.

THE ENTREPRENEUR'S ROLE

"I didn't even know what the word 'entrepreneur' meant until I was a freshman in college. Once I learned about the world of entrepreneurship, I knew, 'This is for me.'"

LAUREN AMARANTE
Co-Founder of World Entrepreneurship Day

When you think of a business owner, you probably imagine a 70-year-old man with an apron who still stands behind the counter at his hardware store. He gets there every day at six in the morning and doesn't leave until ten at night. I'm not sure about you, but that's not what I want.

According to *eMyth*, a world-renowned book on entrepreneurship, there are three levels to business ownership. If you want to become an entrepreneur, you need to work through all three.

1. **The Technician.**
   Also known as the freelancer. They do everything. The technician starts the business, reaches the customers, provides the service, sends the invoice, manages the money,

and never grows. This business owner works 12-hour days and gets paid a little more than your average Joe. Most "entrepreneurs" are technicians.

2. **The Manager.**
    The second level is the manager. They hire people (technicians) to do the day-to-day tasks so they can focus on developing the business. This business owner can work relatively normal hours and generally makes a decent salary because the business is growing.

3. **The Entrepreneur.**
    This is the tycoon of trade, the holy grail of business ownership. Entrepreneurs hire managers to supervise the technicians who do the work. That way, they can step away from the business, still make money, and have complete freedom.

Freedom is the biggest benefit to entrepreneurship. But most "entrepreneurs" never get to enjoy it.

Catherine Cook (20) and Juliette Brindak (21) are two young entrepreneurs who have reached the third level of entrepreneurship. They're both full-time college students who go to school thousands of miles away from the headquarters of their companies. However, both dedicate their spare time to the business and visit as often as they can.

THE ONLY 5 WAYS TO GROW

"Basically, I started out not knowing much and I just kept learning as I went along. That's the biggest thing: always learn, change, and grow with your business."

BEN WEISSENSTEIN
Founder of Grand Slam Garage Sales

Do you want to take a guess at the five ways to grow a business? Go ahead. I'll be here when you get back.

1. Become More Efficient

When you become more efficient, you decrease your costs. By decreasing your costs you increase your profits. The result? Your business grows.

- **Develop better systems.**
  The invention of the assembly line has had a greater impact on the world than the founding of Ford, one of the biggest companies ever. That's the value of systemizing work. If you develop better systems, you'll become more efficient.

- **Buy better equipment.**
  The other way to become more efficient is to invest in better equipment. Systems can only help so much if you don't have the right tools.

- **Make a just noticeable difference.**
  Have you gotten a 99¢ hamburger from Wendy's lately? In order to keep the price at 99 cents, they had to make them just noticeably smaller. A lot of companies do this but you shouldn't.

Emil Motycka got an $8,000 loan at 13 years old so he could buy a commercial mower for his business. Even though it took two years to pay off, he couldn't have grown without it. Now he owns five trucks, two trailers, and about a dozen mowers.

2. Provide Higher Quality

So you can justify an increase in prices. Generally, you should only increase your prices to existing customers if you've upgraded your product or started offering a superior service.

- **Utilize more skilled labor.**
  If you're providing a service, train yourself or find someone to provide the service at a higher quality.

146

- **Offer a better product or upgrade.**
  Either make your existing product better or create another product as an upgrade. This could be as simple as offering your product in a larger size.

Sometimes you can justify a price increase for inflation, but you'll have to deal with backlash from your existing customers.

> One of the reasons Jacob Cass can charge $6000+ for a brand identity is because he has fine-tuned his skills by working with hundreds of clients. Plus, he's won dozens of awards and become one of the most recognized designers in the world. Companies with big budgets will pay for that.

3. Get More Customers

Only get more customers if your business is at a point where it can handle more business.

- **Boost your marketing.**
  Offer a referral program. Pay for advertising. Send out direct mail. Start making sales calls. Get a blog and implement a content marketing strategy. Brainstorm creative ways to get more customers and act on those ideas. To find out how to develop an online content marketing strategy, check out 14clicks.com/click3.

- **Collaborate with complementary businesses.**
  Another way to get more customers is to tap into other businesses' customers. If you're a designer, connect with a developer. If you sell an entrepreneurship eBook, offer an affiliate program to entrepreneurship blogs.

- **Start offering a synergistic product.**
  If you offer a service, the best way to get more customers is to start selling a product that's related to your service. This will expand a previously limited customer base.

Alex Maroko started as a personal trainer. He was maxed out at $15 per hour and could only train people within his community. So he recruited a training expert to develop an athletic training program that he could sell online. He emailed the top basketball training blogs and offered an affiliate commission for them to promote it. In the first week, he made $20K. Over the first five months, he made $100K.

4. Sell More to Existing Customers

One goal with any business is to develop a recurring revenue stream. With a recurring revenue model you can acquire a customer and sell to them on a regular basis, hopefully for life.

- **Offer something that customers keep needing.**
  Deodorant and ice cream are examples of products that customers consume immediately and need to purchase again.

- **Offer complementary services or products.**
  A customer who needs their lawn mowed also needs their sprinklers blown out, leaves picked up, snow removed, and gardens tended. And a basketball player who purchases a training program to become quicker also needs to jump higher and shoot more accurately.

Once you have a list of customers who trust what you sell, you can sell things to them for the rest of your life.

Adam Horwitz has more than 150K email addresses from people who have either bought something or opted-in on one of his websites. He said having this list is, "pretty much like having a virtual ATM."

5. Acquisition

Buy out smaller companies. Once you build your business with good systems and a solid customer base, you can grow strategically by acquiring other businesses.

- **Acquire a service.**
  If you're offering a regional service and you're looking to expand to neighboring regions, it's impractical to try and pick up those customers one at a time. It's not worth the gas and travel time to service one customer. The best way to expand is to purchase a smaller company in that region so you can start with enough customers to make it worthwhile.

- **Buy out a complementary product.**
  Or let's say you've developed software to help small business owners. A bunch of your customers keep requesting an upgrade to the software that will allow additional functionality. Instead of developing it from scratch, look for another company that has developed software that you can integrate with your existing product.

When acquiring another business, start with a reasonable offer so they know you're serious, but leave room to negotiate.

Emil Motycka runs a lawn maintenance company, a gardening company, a snow removal company, and a commercial cleaning company. Towards the end of the mowing season he looks for small mowing operations to acquire because that's when people are looking to sell. Occasionally he'll buy out high school lawn businesses for almost nothing because the owner is going to college.

Sell razor blades, not razors. Sell printer cartridges, not printers. Sell calling plans, not phones. For instance, let's say you buy a $100 iPhone and a $50 per month Verizon calling plan. For the calling plan, you're paying $600 per year and about $25K over the course of your life. The lifetime value (LTV) of a customer for Verizon is about $25K while it's only $1-5K for Apple.

RECRUIT YOUR EMPLOYEES

*"As young people, we think that we're all
superheroes and we can do everything.
Sometimes being young, being
ambitious, and trying to do
everything can hurt you."*

KEITH J. DAVIS JR.
19-Year-Old Professional Speaker, Actor, Model, and Author

A man pushed his car to a hotel and lost his fortune. What happened?

That's one of the interview questions you can expect if you're applying for a software engineering job at Google.

Companies need to hire smart people. A bad hire is one of the most costly mistakes that they make. According to LeapFrog, it costs an average of $4,800 to train a new employee. That includes the time it takes for them to learn their job and your time as the manager to train them.

Once you start hiring, it's important to find the right people who fit with your organization.

Answer: He landed on Boardwalk.

Outsource to Independent Contractors

Before you start hiring employees, get your feet wet by outsourcing to independent contractors.

Independent contractors are freelancers for businesses. But they can only be classified as contractors if they supply the service with their own equipment (e.g. computer, software, tools, etc.). They're like employees in that you pay them to do something for you, but the laws and taxes are much less complicated.

The independent contractor is responsible for sending you their invoices. At the end of the year, you just need to send a 1099 Form to your contractor so they can file their taxes.

With employees, you're responsible for providing regular paychecks. You also have to withhold Social Security and Medicare taxes on the employee's behalf and pay those taxes for each of them at the end of the year.

To find independent contractors, go to www.Elance.com.

> When a big snow storm hits in Northern Colorado, Emil Motycka can't clear all his snow contracts himself. So he has a network of about 65 independent contractors. Then they invoice him and he sends them 1099's at the end of the year.

Find Employees

With unemployment at 10%, there millions of people looking for jobs so it should be easy to find them, right? Kinda. There are lots of people looking for jobs but it's still hard to find and qualify the right people.

Here are a few places to post jobs and find employees:

- **Networking.**
  Most jobs come through your network. That's because business owners hire the people they already know and the people they're referred to. When your friend refers you to a potential employee, that friend is putting their reputation on the line. It's a good way to easily find people and pre-qualify your workforce.

- **Craigslist.**
  In general, these aren't going to be highly-educated employees but they'll appreciate the job and work really hard.

- **Industry Job Boards.**
  People who are looking for specific jobs will post their résumés on industry websites (e.g. Monster.com, CareerBuilder.com, etc.). Plus, most of these sites let you post jobs to help them find you.

- **University Job Postings.**
  You can hire college students as interns but you're not going to attract the good ones unless you pay them. Interns have a solid education and a quick learning curve.

- **Technical Schools.**
  One of the most untapped sources of quality labor is technical schools. There are high school and college programs across the country that train people how to perform certain skills (e.g. automotive technicians, graphic designers, videographers, web developers, etc.). Contact them and see if they can send one of their best students your way.

Once you find a qualified employee, take the time to interview them. A short conversation will tell you a lot about that person's work ethic and career aspirations.

Emil Motycka finds most of the workers for his maintenance company on Craigslist.com. He tried hiring his friends and fellow college students, but they don't work as hard. He told me that he always wants to hire blue-collar workers because they're not entitled and stuck up like people with college degrees.

Hiring and Training

Always hire character and train skill. You can look at a résumé or portfolio in ten seconds and figure out if they're qualified for the job. But that doesn't mean that they're a good fit for your company.

The purpose of an interview is to judge the character of a person. Once you find someone with a solid character who wants to work for you, they're going to learn quickly and work hard.

When you bring your first employee on board, spend a week or so showing them everything about your operation and training them on their role. If that person works out, have them train all the other employees that you hire.

Joe Penna, the 6th most subscribed YouTuber, hired a college intern to help him capture the footage and do a rough cut so he can start working on the music and concepts. He also enlists the help of his fiancé to make a lot of his videos.

Promote From Within

Once your business is at the point where you have too many employees to manage yourself, it's time to promote one of them to a managerial position.

If you believe a current employee can do a sufficient job of managing everyone else, promote from within. This will show the other employees that they have the ability to move up in your organization and it will make everyone work harder. Ultimately, it's your decision who you promote, but it's best to get all of your employees on board with your decision before you make it.

Another option is to hire an outsider with management experience, but that person is going to have a hard time gaining the respect from the current employees.

Emil Motycka has had one solid, dependable employee working for him for the past couple years. Last summer he promoted that person to Foreman. Now he is responsible for managing all the other employees while they're out in the field and Emil is behind a desk.

Get a Personal Assistant

After you fill a management position or two, the next step is to get a personal assistant. Someone to help you do the monotonous portions of your job (emails, phone calls, data entry, etc.).

Personal assistants cost anywhere from $20-50 per hour. If you can get that much value out of being able to do the high-impact tasks, then it's a no-brainer.

If you need a personal assistant before you have office space, get a virtual assistant. Find an affordable virtual assistant on Elance.com.

Joe Penna's second hire was a personal assistant to wade through his emails, keep track of his schedule, and run his errands. This gives him more time to focus on what he loves: making kooky videos

Payroll

If you only hire out to independent contractors, payroll is simple. Pay them when they send you an invoice.

When you have employees who work regular hours for you, pay them every two weeks. This is manageable for you and it lets them take care of their bills. It's easy to keep track of your staff and their hours with your FreshBooks.com account that you should have set up by now.

It's important to note that if you have an employee who works more than 12 hours in a day or 40 hours in a week, you have to pay them time-and-a-half for overtime, which is 150% of their normal wage. You can also choose to pay your employees time-and-a-half if they work holidays.

Syed Balkhi has a small team of four people on his payroll for Uzzz.net. Last year he netted $600,000 with that company. When I asked how he pays his employees, he said, "Honestly, I have no clue. I'm not the business guy. I let my CPA (Certified Public Accountant) take care of all that."

Firing

A bad employee can have more of a negative effect than a few missed deadlines and missing lunches. When you have an employee with a negative attitude, that individual will bring down everybody in your organization.

In most cases, if you want to fire someone, you need to have just cause. This means you need to document everything your employees do wrong so if you decide to fire them, you'll have documentation to show why. This is a burden.

Some states are Employment at Will. This means you can fire employees without a reason at anytime. It's good for employers but it can be stressful for employees. Although the good employees should know that they have nothing to worry about.

> Emil Motycka hired the buddy of one of his employees because he figured they would work well together. Instead, they goofed off and it almost toppled his business. He fired the guy and set a policy to not let friends work together.

> Focus on hiring the right people from the outset and reduce employee turnover by creating a culture that keeps people in your company.

FIND SPACE TO WORK

"We have 80 employees but we are very tightly knit. It's a high-energy office, but we all hang out together."

CATHERINE COOK
Co-Founder of myYearbook

You've been bootstrapping, right?

Up until now, you should have been working from home, coffee shops, or out in the field. Once you can afford working space, start looking.

Coworking Habitats

This is a new trend that's starting up across America. People are leasing office buildings then subleasing individual offices to entrepreneurs. It's called "coworking" and I'm a big fan.

It's hard to hold yourself accountable as a solo entrepreneur. By working in a coworking environment, you'll be amongst other self-motivated people who you can feed off of. Not to mention, someone to eat lunch with.

Paying a couple hundred bucks a month to rent an office when you can work from home or a coffee shop may seem like a raw deal, but it's not when you consider that most offices cost thousands per month.

To find a local coworking office, search for "coworking space (your city)."

Jacob Cass could easily sustain himself with his design jobs for a long time, but he decided to take a salaried job in New York City. Part of the reason is just so he could work in an office environment with other motivated people.

Incubate Me

Incubating is the next step up from coworking. Small business incubators are meant to facilitate entrepreneurs by offering low-cost office space with access to professional advice.

Like coworking spaces, entrepreneurship incubators are popping up everywhere as the government starts to realize the value in helping entrepreneurs.

Most incubators have an application process because they only want to accept entrepreneurs that have potential to become substantial businesses. Typically, incubators are three-to-six-month programs.

To find a local incubator through the National Business Incubation Association, go to www.NBIA.org.

TechStars.org is the #1 startup incubator in the nation. It's like the entrepreneur's equivalent of getting into Stanford. They're located in Boston, Boulder, Seattle, and NYC. They've only been around for three years and have had 39 companies go through the program. Out of those 39 companies, five have been acquired for more than $2M and 27 have gotten funding or hit profitability.

Office Space

Once you start collecting employees, it's impractical to fit everyone into a coworking space and your incubator time is probably up. It's time to move into an office of your own.

The general rule is that you need between 175 and 250 square feet of office space for every person working there. Commercial office leases range from $25-$45 per square foot per year. So a 1,500 square foot office will cost about $35,000 per year or $3,000 per month. If you can't afford that yet, you shouldn't be hiring in the first place.

To find affordable commercial office space, go to www.LoopNet.com.

myYearbook.com is headquartered in New Hope, Pennsylvania. When they started, Catherine Cook and crew leased out a relatively small office. As the company grew, they had to hire contractors to turn neighboring retail space into office space. Now they have 80 employees.

Warehouse It

Employees aren't the only part of your business that you need to make room for. If you have a lot of equipment or inventory, eventually you'll need to find a warehouse.

Warehouses typically cost $3-$10 per square foot per year. So a 5,000 square foot warehouse might cost you $30,000 per year. The benefit to warehousing your equipment is that it'll last longer and maintain its value. The benefit to warehousing your inventory is that it won't clutter your home or office.

To find a local warehouse, go to www.LoopNet.com.

Emil Motycka has five trucks, two trailers, and about a dozen mowers. Not all of his mowers can fit in his trailers so he bought a building for $3,000 that he can assemble on his property. It has the same effect as a warehouse, but it's much cheaper.

Retail Space

Let's say you want to sell your products the old-fashioned way: in your own store. Then you'll need to get retail space.

Depending on the location, size, and a slew of other factors, retail space runs $10-$100 per square foot per year. Generally it's in the $10-20 range. A 1,500 square foot store is pretty standard and that'll cost around $23,000 per year. Then utilities will cost another couple hundred bucks per month. And a five-person staff will run you about another $100,000.

If you can make an extra $125,000 per year with a store, go for it. Otherwise, stick to the internet.

Johnny Earle, the 28-year-old founder of Johnny Cupcakes, started his t-shirt business in 2001. He pledged to stay out of retail chains so he could focus on building a brand. Now he has three stores across the nation and he hit revenues of $3.8 million in 2008. As part of his brand all of his stores are made-out to look like bakeries, even though he doesn't sell cupcakes.

The Johnny Cupcakes store in LA.

> If you're looking for a small office, maybe for you and a handful of employees, look for a space that has shared access to a receptionist, a conference room, a kitchen, and a print/copy center. When clients come to visit, they'll be impressed.

EXIT THE BUSINESS

"I love the internet and I will always work with it, but my ultimate goal is to build casinos, hotels, and nightclubs. I want to be a skyscraper guy."

ANDREW FASHION
Made $2.5 Million by 21

Steve Jobs has an annual salary of $1.

Entrepreneurs love their companies so much that they'd rather reinvest money in the business than give themselves a proper salary. Rarely do they get big pay days until they sell the business.

Build a company that you can sell. But that can be hard too.

After he sold his company in 1992, Richard Branson was seen crying while walking down the street holding a $1 Billion check.

Sell the Business

If you do a good job of building and marketing your business, you're going to have people approach you all the time wanting to buy it. Depending on the amount of recurring revenue and rate of growth, the price tag for a business should be set at one-to-three year's revenue.

If you're looking to sell a small operation, post it on Craigslist and other industry forums. Entrepreneurs are always looking to acquire small businesses and that's where they look.

No matter how you try to sell your business, make them set the first offer. This lets you know how serious they are and what sort of budget they have. If you make the first offer, you give them all the negotiating power.

Last summer, Emil Motycka was running at about 100 lawns per week and out of curiosity he posted the business for sale on Craigslist. Within 24 hours, he had three offers to buy it. All over six-figures.

Sell a Website

Selling a website is easier because you can sell it to anyone, anywhere. Just provide the stats and potential buyers run them through their software to pump out a valuation.

Current revenue, PageRank, Alexa Rank, inbound links, unique visitors, pageviews, size of email list, open rates, click through rates, number of Facebook fans, and number of Twitter followers all factor in to how much your site is worth.

The easiest way to sell your website is to post it on Flippa.com, the #1 marketplace for buying and selling websites. They're about to surpass $50M in all-time website sales with 62% of those sold in the last three months.

List your website and decide if you want it to be an auction with a reserve or if you want to review private offers. They have 400K unique visitors per month who take a look, place a bid, or make an offer. Then you decide if you want to sell.

To list your website on Flippa, go to www.Flippa.com.

For the first year that he ran WPBeginner.com, Syed Balkhi didn't put his name anywhere on the site. Part of the reason is that he wanted to build a community based on the quality of the content and not on how much they liked the author. Once your name becomes synonymous with your business, it becomes less appealing to someone who might want to buy it. Buyers know they're going to lose a lot of the community when the owner leaves. On the other hand, Syed's site has grown even larger now that his community knows who is behind it.

> If you're trying to build a business to sell, focus on getting recurring revenue. A company with $100,000 in annual revenue that has monthly customers is more valuable than a company that makes $1 million in annual revenue selling something that people only purchase once.

GIVE BACK

"My preliminary life goal is to donate 80% to humanitarian aid and research. Since my career goal is to earn $10 billion, that would be $8 billion."

MARK BAO
11 Companies and 3 Foundations by 17

In 2010, Warren Buffet and Bill Gates set out to convince America's billionaires to pledge 50% of their fortunes to charity. So far they've recruited 57 of the about 400 billionaires. This commitment titled, *The Giving Pledge*, could potentially contribute $600B back to the world.

But you don't have to be rich to give back. In fact, their generosity is part of the reason many of them made $1,000,000,000 in the first place.

Support a Cause from the Outset

One option you have for giving back is to commit a portion of your profits to charity. Lots of companies are starting to do this but very few have done it from day one.

Besides just doing a good thing for society, it's good for marketing as well. Customers are more likely to purchase from a socially responsible business and the companies that support a cause tend to get more press.

If you're doing it for business reasons, that's fine. Just make sure that you're supporting a cause that your target market wants to support. For instance, don't support PETA if you sell camouflage.

They're competing with Nike and Zappos, but TOMS Shoes has found a philanthropic way to stick out. For every pair of shoes that TOMS sells, they give another pair to a child in need. When you buy a pair of TOMS Shoes, you're buying into a movement, you're changing a life. I want to be reminded that I changed a life every time I put on my shoes.

Commit to Donate Long-Term

If it doesn't make sense to commit a portion of your profits to charity, at least commit to donating in the long-term. There's nothing wrong with saying that you'll support a cause once you reach a certain level of comfortability with your own life.

In fact, deciding to keep the money in the business to help it grow so you have more money to donate down the road is ultimately better for society. That is, if you decide that your business will do better if it keeps the money.

As you saw in his quote, Mark Bao has publicly pledged to donate 80% of his life earnings back to humanitarian aid and research. Not many 17-year-olds have done that.

Invest in Entrepreneurs

When people choose to donate, they automatically think, "I should give to a non-profit."

Guess what? Startup companies need that money just as much if not more. And businesses contribute back to society much more than most non-profits. Nothing burns through money faster than an organization that doesn't need to be fiscally-responsible to survive (send your angry emails to nick@14clicks.com).

So, if you become inconceivably wealthy, like I expect you to, I challenge you to give most of that money back to entrepreneurs. Just imagine if someone came along and gave you $100,000 right now to start your business.

I was reading the blog of a venture capitalist the other day and realized that my ultimate goal in life is to become a VC. I've got an idea (not 14 Clicks) that could easily become an eight-figure exit. If I'm as smart as I think I am, then this would let me invest in young entrepreneurs for the rest of my life. I'd get to work with passionate entrepreneurs everyday and I'd be able to relax by spreading my risk across multiple ventures. It's exactly what I want my life to be.

> Kids who grow up in wealthy families tend to act snobbish, be lazy, and feel entitled. Give your fortune to someone who deserves it.

Bonus

61 STEPS

TO BECOMING A SUCCESSFUL YOUNG ENTREPRENEUR

"Start today, not tomorrow. If anything, you should have started yesterday."

EMIL MOTYCKA

From 'Mow Boy' to $250K

There's a thousand different ways to get from New York City to Los Angeles. Some ways are relatively easy while others are full of obstacles. But no matter how you get there, you still have to cross the Mississippi and scale the Rockies.

Similarly, there's no such thing as a set path to entrepreneurial success, but you do need to be headed in the right direction.

Some overnight successes take just a few years, while other entrepreneurs run in circles for decades. Before you find success, there are certain things that you need to do and a certain order in which you need to do them.

Follow these 61 steps for the most obstacle-free path to becoming a successful young entrepreneur.

HAVE AN IDEA

"To be successful, you have to have your heart in your business, and your business in your heart."

THOMAS J. WATSON
Founder of IBM

1. **Come up with your idea.**
   The first thing you need is a problem that you're passionate about solving. Then build a business on top of that solution.

2. **Package your idea as a service if you can.**
   Services are easier to start because you can make money right away. Products require extensive research, product development, manufacturing, and distribution. Then when you sell it, it might be months before you get paid. However, products are easier to scale. Start as a service then expand into a product.

KNOW THE ROPES

*"Whenever you are asked if you can do a job,
tell 'em. 'Certainly, I can!' Then get busy
and find out how to do it."*

THEODORE ROOSEVELT
Former U.S. President

3. **Google your business idea.**
To find other people and businesses doing what you want to do. Write down those keywords because that's how people will find your business.

4. **Question why it hasn't been done before.**
If you can't find anyone, you have a first-mover advantage. But you need to ask yourself why no one else is doing it. Find the answer to that question before you move forward.

5. **Learn from your competitors.**
If you find competitors, you'll be able to learn from them. Take a look at every detail of their business and, if you want to be bold, call them up and ask questions.

6. **Find a mentor.**
A good mentor will save you years-worth of mistakes. Contact the leader in your field and see if they'll mentor you. You might have to start that relationship by doing something for them.

7. **Fly solo or recruit a team.**
It's best to start by yourself. But if you need a team, you'll have to compensate them fairly with ownership in the company. Then set roles and expectations for those roles.

PLAN YOUR SUCCESS

"In preparing for battle I have always found that plans are useless, but planning is indispensable."

DWIGHT D. EISENHOWER
Former Five-Star General and U.S. President

8. **Determine the problem you're solving.**
   This is the most important thing to know about your business. Everything you do from here on out will work towards solving this problem.

9. **Figure out exactly what you're selling.**
   You're getting paid for your product or service, but that's not what you're selling. You need to sell the benefits to what you're offering. Sell them on how you can solve their problem.

10. **Research your service or develop your product.**
    Find out how other companies are providing their product or service. Learn from their business and everything that they're doing. Then replicate their success.

11. **Calculate your startup costs.**
    You need to know exactly how much you need to get started. Once you have a number written down, double it. You will have unexpected expenses.

12. **Settle on your pricing.**
    One way to price is to determine your total costs per unit. Then simply mark it up. A better way to price is to figure out the real value to your customers and price it accordingly.

MARKET YOUR BUSINESS

"Your most unhappy customers are your
greatest source of learning."

BILL GATES
Wealthiest Person in the World

13. Select a niche target market.
The smaller your target market, the more easily you'll be able to find and reach them. Choose the absolute best customer and only appeal to that type of person.

14. Name your company.
Use a brandable name like Google if you're trying to appeal to consumers (B2C). Use a generic name like International Business Machines (IBM) if your target market is other businesses (B2B).

15. Tagline your company.
Once you have the name, craft a tagline or catchphrase that sums up and explains the key benefits to your company. "Just do it."

16. Establish a brand message.
What do you want your customers to think of when they hear about or see your company? That message should be woven into everything that represents your business. It's called a brand.

17. Choose your company colors.
Research the psychology of colors to determine which colors will best represent your brand. Blue is popular for businesses because it's gender neutral and it signifies trust. Red is used a lot by restaurants because it attracts the eye more than any other color.

169

18. **Get a logo.**

Unless you're a graphic designer, your logo is the first thing you should outsource for your business. The software alone costs $700 to make a looking logo. 99designs.com is a relatively inexpensive way to get a great logo.

REACH YOUR CUSTOMERS

"One can get anything if he is willing to help enough others get what they want."

ZIG ZIGLAR
Author and Motivational Speaker

19. **Get business cards.**

You need business cards. You can get 250 generic, "free" business cards from Vistaprint,com for about $8 (pay for shipping). If you go with a local printer, they'll charge about $80 for 250 business cards.

20. **Sharpen your elevator pitch.**

Before you start networking, you need to know what you're going to say when someone asks, "What do you do?" Your response should be a 60-second elevator pitch.

21. **Attend a local entrepreneurship networking event.**

The first group of people that you should meet is your local entrepreneurs. These people will introduce you to other important people in the business community. Find a local entrepreneurship networking event on Meetup.com.

22. **Choose the best way to contact potential customers.**

Advertize to your customers how they want to be advertized to. Choose between meeting them face-to-face, cold-calling, email, direct mail, posters or flyers, online job postings, or driving traffic to your website.

23. Nail down your sales pitch.

Once you know how you're going to reach them, you have to figure out what to say. Use the golden structure for getting someone to purchase no matter what channel you choose.

24. Make your marketing materials.

Now you need to create your marketing materials. Maybe it's print advertising, a sales pitch script, a sales page, or a sales video.

LIFT OFF

"The true entrepreneur is a doer, not a dreamer."

NOLAN BUSHNELL

Founder of Atari and Chuck E. Cheese's

25. Create a system for fulfilling orders.

Before you launch, you need to know how you're going to supply what you sell. Gather your initial inventory or set a process for providing the service.

26. Get a way to accept payments.

Cash-only doesn't cut it anymore. You need to be able to accept checks and credit cards. Use SquareUp.com if you're accepting credit cards in person. Use Shopify.com or GetShopped.org (if WordPress) as your online shopping cart.

27. Launch your business offline.

If your business is primarily offline, start by recruiting customers from your neighborhood or local community. You can do this with flyers, press releases, partnerships, or good ol' fashion phone calls.

28. Launch your website or blog.

If you're launching an online service, all you need is a WordPress website with your About, Contact, Services, and Portfolio pages. If you're launching a product, launch it through targeted press or affiliates. If you're launching a blog, soft launch it with five articles and do a big launch once you have 20. To find more details about this process, check out www.14clicks.com/click3.

GET IT DONE

"An entrepreneur tends to bite off a little more than he can chew hoping he'll quickly learn how to chew it."

ROY ASH

Former Director of the U.S. Office of Management and Budget

29. **Set SMART goals.**

Your goals should be specific, measurable, achievable, relevant, and time-bound. Set one-year, six-month, three-month, and one-month goals.

30. **Establish weekly and daily tasks.**

From your goals, set weekly and daily tasks based on the projects you need to get done in the order you need to do them.

31. **Get a planner.**

At the beginning of the week, set a to-do list for every day. Write that to-do list in your planner so you can open it up in the morning and know exactly what you need to get done.

32. **Start a business idea notebook.**

Designate a notebook for all of your miscellaneous business thoughts. Take it everywhere to collect all of your ideas in one place.

33. **Land a customer.**

To land your first customer, start by bidding on a job or making an offer. If you win the bid, set expectations for your client.

Negotiate the terms of the contract. Sign the contract. Bam, you're hired.

34. Provide the service or deliver the product.

Have a repeatable system for delivering the service that you can easily train to future employees. If you sell a product, set a process for delivering that product as efficiently as possible.

35. Focus on productivity.

Keep in mind that you're only making money for the time that you're producing or selling something. Schedule an hour in the morning for phone calls and an hour at night for emails. Then you have the heart of the day to focus on the heart of your business.

36. Organize and track your business.

FreshBooks.com lets you easily create projects, track time for individual projects, professionally invoice your customers, and pay your staff.

37. Be remarkable.

According to NOP World, 93% of customers identified word of mouth as the best, most reliable source of information they use to make purchasing decisions. Encourage word of mouth from your customers by being interesting, providing referral incentives, and making yourself sharable.

FIND YOUR FORTUNE

"The greatest reward in becoming a millionaire is not the amount of money that you earn. It is the kind of person that you have to become to become a millionaire in the first place."

JIM ROHN
Entrepreneur, Author, and Motivational Speaker

38. **Design your business for cash flow.**

    As an entrepreneur, sometimes you'll get paid before you do the work and other times you'll have to wait months to get paid, if at all. Establish a payment policy to get paid as soon as possible.

39. **Collect your money.**

    If you're selling in person, you can accept cash or take credit cards with SquareUp.com. Otherwise you'll have to invoice your client with flexible payment terms. FreshBooks.com lets you easily send a professional invoice via snail mail or email.

40. **Track your earnings.**

    In the beginning, you should track your revenues and expenses in a simple Excel spreadsheet. Or you can use FreshBooks.com to track every dollar and run reports on your earnings. If you haven't noticed, FreshBooks is pretty much the greatest tool out there for entrepreneurs.

41. **Reinvest or pay yourself.**

    Once your business becomes profitable, you have to decide if you want to reinvest that money to grow, or you can pay yourself and stay flat.

42. **Find an investor if you need one.**

    Only on rare occasions should you look for an investor. Good investors only invest in companies that have already made money and are looking for cash to make big moves.

LEGAL MUMBO JUMBO

*"Leadership is doing what is right
when no one is watching."*

GEORGE VAN VALKENBURG
Entrepreneur, Inventor, Author, and Speaker

43. **Get your vendor's license.**
If you're selling a product in person, you'll need a vendor's license. They cost about $25 and you get them from your local government.

44. **File a provisional application for patent.**
If you have an invention you want to protect, start by filling a provisional application for patent with the US Patent and Trademark Office at www.USPTO.gov.

45. **Reserve your trade name.**
Your trade name is your business name. It's also known as, "Doing business as..." If you're going to register your company, first you need to reserve your trade name.

46. **Register your Limited Liability Company (LLC).**
To become a bona fide company, you need to register your business with your state's Secretary of State. Most states let you do this online and charge an average of $25-100.

47. **Get your Employer Identification Number (EIN).**
Your EIN is like a social security number for your company. They're free and you can get yours at IRS.gov.

48. **Set up a business bank account.**
Every entrepreneur needs a business bank account. Most banks require that you have an LLC and an EIN. Always separate your personal expenses from your business expenses by using your business credit or debit card.

49. **Figure out if you need insurance.**
Most entrepreneurs won't need additional insurance. But if you're operating in a hazardous work environment or have lots of expensive equipment, it's worth the extra $100 per month to pick up general liability insurance.

50. Set aside money for taxes.

Keep 25-30% of your profits in your business savings account to pay taxes at the end of the year.

51. Schedule meetings with a Certified Public Accountant (CPA) and a small business lawyer.

Eventually you'll need to hire a CPA and/or a small business lawyer. It's best to start cultivating these relationships early on so maybe one day they'll give you a deal. Plus, the first meeting should be free. Take advantage of it.

GROW

*"Entrepreneurship is living a few years of your life
like most people won't, so that you can spend
the rest of your life like most people can't."*

ANONYMOUS

A Student in an Entrepreneurship Class

52. Become more efficient.

The easiest way to grow your business is to become more efficient. This reduces your costs and increases your profit margins. The best two ways to become more efficient are to develop better systems or buy better equipment.

53. Boost your marketing.

Another way to grow is to get more customers. You do that by boosting your marketing. Offer a referral program, pay for advertising, send out direct mail, make sales calls, or find a creative way to reach more potential customers.

54. Complement your product line or service offering.

A third way to grow is to sell more to existing customers. Do that by developing and offering complementary products and services.

55. **Outsource to independent contractors.**
Before you hire employees, get your feet wet by outsourcing to independent contractors. Legally, they're a lot less complicated than employees. But they won't be loyal to you and your business unless you give them a full-time position.

56. **Hire employees.**
Once you're up to speed with hiring practices, bring a few employees onboard. Start by asking your independent contractors if they'd like a more permanent position. Then ask for employee referrals, look on job boards, and reach out to your local school systems.

57. **Find space to work.**
As you bring workers in-house, you'll need to move your business out of your house. Office space usually costs about $25-$45 per square foot per year. Warehouses generally cost $3-$10 per square foot per year. If you want to open a store, retail space costs $10-$100 per square foot per year.

58. **Hire managers.**
After you're moved in and your employees are self-sufficient, it's time to find a manager or two. Start by promoting within if you have good candidates. This will let you step out of the business and into the "entrepreneur" role.

59. **Sell the business.**
If you want to get out of the business completely, it's time to sell. Assuming you built a business with recurring revenue, it'll be worth one-to-three years' revenue. Post your business for sale on Craigslist and industry forums. That's where other entrepreneurs are looking to acquire.

60. **Take a vacation.**
Either that or dive into another venture.

61. **Give back.**

Most people only consider non-profits when they think of charitable giving, but I want to give back to entrepreneurs. Give your fortune to whoever you want. Just make sure it's someone or something that deserves it.

ABOUT
NICHOLAS TART

I'm a 22-year-old, full-time entrepreneur living in Colorado.

My companies include JuniorBiz and 14 Clicks and I'm the co-author of What it Takes to Make More Money than Your Parents.

I graduated Magna Cum Laude from Colorado State University in 2010 and I have dedicated my career to teaching and helping young entrepreneurs.

NICHOLAS TART
Founder of 14 Clicks

ACKNOWLEDGE
NICK SCHEIDIES

Nick Scheidies is a 22-year-old, entrepreneur from Colorado. He contributed by writing and editing portions of this book and by helping me lay the foundation for 14 Clicks.

He is one of the few people who has worked with me and encouraged me to pursue my unrealistic dream of becoming a successful entrepreneur. I'm grateful for his help, support, and friendship.

Now Nick is continuing his entrepreneurship with Newborn: a creative collective that sees the world with fresh eyes.

NICK SCHEIDIES
Founder of Newborn Collective

CLICK 2
GET INSPIRED BY THE TOP YOUNG ENTREPRENEURS

You may have noticed that there are a lot of inspirational and practical quotes in this book. That's because there are two things you need to have to be successful:

1. *Know-how. I wrote this book to give you the know-how. But just because you know how to do something, doesn't mean you'll do it.*

2. *Motivation. I wrote another book that'll inspire and motivate you more than anything. It has interviews with 25 of the world's top young entrepreneurs ages 12-23 who candidly shared the secrets to their success.*

In fact, most of the quotes in this book are from our young entrepreneurs in What it Takes to Make More Money than Your Parents. To get inspired by the planet's top young entrepreneurs, go to:

www.14clicks.com/click2

CLICK 3
CREATE A WEBSITE THAT MAKES YOUR BUSINESS MORE MONEY

No matter what type of business you have, you need to be online. But you probably don't have a clue where to start.

That's why I've put together a course to teach you how to:

- ✔ *Save $18.95* on your domain and hosting.

- ✔ *Install, setup, and optimize* a WordPress site.

- ✔ Get on the *1st page of Google* almost every time.

- ✔ Integrate Facebook and Twitter to *go viral*.

- ✔ Implement a content strategy to get *free traffic*.

- ✔ Convert your traffic into *paying customers*.

- ✔ Make money online with *four fool-proof systems*.

To create a money-making machine for your business, go to:

www.14clicks.com/click3

www.ingramcontent.com/pod-product-compliance
Lightning Source LLC
Chambersburg PA
CBHW060556200326
41521CB00007B/587